William Cullen Bryant

Letters from the East

William Cullen Bryant
Letters from the East
ISBN/EAN: 9783744711166

Printed in Europe, USA, Canada, Australia, Japan

Cover: Foto ©ninafisch / pixelio.de

More available books at **www.hansebooks.com**

LETTERS FROM THE EAST.

BY

WILLIAM CULLEN BRYANT.

NEW YORK:
G. P. PUTNAM & SON.
1869.

Entered according to Act of Congress, in the year 1869,
BY WM. CULLEN BRYANT,
In the Clerk's office of the District Court of the United States for the Southern District of New York.

Stereotyped by LITTLE, RENNIE & CO.,
645 & 647 Broadway, New York.

TO THE READER.

THE Letters which form the contents of this volume were written in the course of a visit made to the Old World in the closing months of the year 1852, and the first six months of the year following. The author has been induced to collect and present them in this form by the encouragement of the Publisher, who thought that the volume might be fortunate enough to find readers.

NEW YORK, *September* 1, 1869.

CONTENTS.

LETTER I.

Contraband books.—Strictness of the Custom-house Officers.—Captain Lynch and his book.—Poetry in the Custom-house.—England deluged with rain.—Prosperity of England in 1852.—Emigration to Australia.................... 9

LETTER II.

Return of gayety and commercial activity in Paris.—The *Credit Mobilier.*—The Empire succeeding a Republic which has lost its liberties. The new Emperor conducted to the Tuileries.—Absence of enthusiasm in the people.—Motives of those who voted for the Empire.—Acquiescence of all parties in the Empire.—Huntington the artist...... 16

LETTER III.

Nismes, its Roman remains, Amphitheatre, Maison Carrée and Pont du Gard.—Amphitheatre at Arles.—The Boulevards.—Roman baths.—Public garden.—Dryness of the climate.—The fountain of the Esplanade.—Delaroche's picture of Cromwell contemplating Charles I. in his coffin..................... 24

LETTER IV.

Security from accident on board the Mediterranean steamers.—Discomforts of a small steamer.—Fine view of the Maritime Alps from the water.—A day in Genoa.—Vexations of the passport system.—Pæstum Amalfi.—Neapolitan boatmen.—Beauty of the coast.—Songs of the boatmen.—Peculiarities of Neapolitan pronunciation.—Excursion to Pæstum.—Sickly inhabitants.—Messina.—Malta.—La Valletta.—The Catholic church in Malta.......................... 34

LETTER V.

Voyage from Malta to Cairo.—A steamer crowded with passengers from England to India.—Ill-bred people.—Fortune, the botanist.—The tea-plant in America and India.—The grape in China and Japan.—A Chinese fruit for America.—A hardy palm.—Arrival at Alexandria.—Confusion of the landing.—Passage to Cairo.—The canal.—the Nile.—Arab devotions.—Youth drowned in the Nile.......... 55

CONTENTS.

LETTER VI.

Sights and sounds of Cairo.—Aspect of the crowd in the streets.—Women.—The bazars.—The barbers.—Mosques.—Noisy habits of the Egyptians.—Mosque of Mohammed Ali.—The pyramids of Ghizeh.—Arab boatmen.—Bedouins.—Purpose of the pyramids.—Pyramids of Sakkara.—M. Mariette and his excavations.—Temple and tomb of Apis.—The site of Memphis.—Mounds of sun-dried brick.—Vast grove of palms.—Saltpetre manufactured from the bricks 69

LETTER VII.

Passage in a steamer up the Nile to Thebes and the lower cataract of the Nile.—Arrangements for the voyage.—Beauty of the weather.—Upper Egypt, its aspect.—Irrigation.—Villages.—Scarcity of fruit-trees.—Rocky hills overlooking the narrow valley of the Nile.—The Temples of Thebes and Karnac.—A French excavator, M. Mounier.—Uncovering of old temples.—Tyranny of the Egyptian authorities.—A Latin convent.—Copts.—Their church 89

LETTER VIII.

Journey from Cairo to Jerusalem across the Little Desert.—Gardens enclosed by the prickly pear.—Olive-trees.—Sycamore of the Virgin.—The Obelisk of Heliopolis.—Village of Khankia.—Lake of the Pilgrims.—Brief twilight.—Journey on camels.—Hoopoes.—Entrance on the Desert.—Our dragoman.—The father of couriers.—Furniture of our caravan.—Ground strewn with fragments of pottery.—An Arab burial-ground.—Village of Belbays 102

LETTER IX.

Second, third, fourth, fifth, and sixth days of our journey.—A visit from two Arab women.—Coquetry of the younger.—Horsemanship of the Arabs.—A belt of cultivation in the Desert.—Rassel Wady.—Flocks of birds.—Irrigation.—Arabs singing.—A dragoman flogs an Arab.—A camel runs away.—A mirage.—Barook.—Pilgrims from Mecca.—A sirocco.—Dead camels.—A monkey digging sorrel.—Violence of the wind.—Our tents overturned at night.—Gatieh.—Personal appearance of the Arabs.—Vermin 113

LETTER X.

Seventh, eighth, and ninth days of our journey.—Bedouin huts.—Women at the hand-mills.—A salt-plain.—Ruins of a tower.—A well in the Desert.—Brackish water.—Arabs amusing themselves with our monkey.—Flocks of goats and sheep.—Importunity of the flies.—We meet a merchants' caravan.—Mosquitoes.—Animal life in the

Desert.—Tracks of jackals and gazelles.—Sight of the Mediterranean.—Shrubs of the Desert.—Minute flowers.—Herd of camels feeding.—Pools of water in the salt-plains.—Springs of mineral oil.—Cry of the jackal.—Town of El Areesh.—Plantations of young palms.—Sand-hills and drifts.—Fruit-trees............................... 127

LETTER XI.

Tenth day of the journey.—Picturesque costumes.—Spirited horses and horsemanship.—Trouble with passports.—Barley-fields.—Women cutting up juniper.—Tributes to the Arabs.—An Arab exquisite.—A pastoral region.—Another tribute.—A salt lake.—Safayda.—Tomb of a Santon.—Flocks of birds.—Frightful scream of a jackal.—Reading the Scriptures.—A troop of dervishes.—An Arab cemetery....... 143

LETTER XII.

Cultivated fields between bare sand-hills.—Ruins of Rhaphia.—The virgin's fountain.—Khan Yoonas.—Fruit-trees in bloom.—Our party in quarantine.—We pass the night in a cemetery.—A crowd of women in white, among the graves.—Oranges.—Distinguished-looking visitors.—Departure from Khan Yoonas.—Pilgrims.—The scarlet anemone.—Old sycamores.—Men ploughing with camels.—We enter the lazaretto at Gaza.—View of the country from our windows.—Foolish look of the dervishes.—Our monkey attacks one of the holy men.—An Arab virago.—Show of tongues.—Release from the lazaretto.. 157

LETTER XIII.

Continuation of the journey to Jerusalem.—The Gate of Gaza.—A vast olive grove.—Curious travelling cradle.—Remains of a Christian church.—Askelon.—Ancient walls.—Sand drifting over the fields.—El Medjal.—Little oxen.—Rude ploughs.—Ashdod.—Ruins of a large Khan.—A chorus of frogs.—Gazelles feeding.—Village of Zebna.—Saracenic bridges.—Women carrying burdens.—Town of Ramleh.—An abandoned tower.—Plain of Sharon.—A convent, where we pass the night.—The mosquitoes from the cisterns.... 168

LETTER XIV.

Journey to Jerusalem continued.—We take our leave of the Arabs and their camels.—Journey on horseback.—Queer bridles and saddles.—A janizary of the American Vice-Consul at Jerusalem.—His long staff.—Entrance upon the hill-country.—A lunch under evergreen oaks.—Steep ascent by a bridle-path.—Sure-footed horses.—Soil full of loose stones.—Its fertility.—First sight of the Holy City.—The

Jaffa gate of the city.—People promenading in the country.—Bearded priests.—Hotel kept by a Maltese.—Visit to the Church of the Holy Sepulchre.. 179

LETTER XV.

The Lazaretto at Smyrna.—Beautiful harbor.—Fleet of American ships of war in the Levant.—Behavior of the Arabs to the Frank.—Relaxation of bigotry.—Mohammedan prejudices.—No Christian converts from Moslems.—Power of the foreign consuls.—Extravagant prerogatives of the American consuls.—Hasty appointments to consulships.—American missionaries at Beyroot.—Dr. Eli Smith.—Mr. Calhoun.—A Druse Emir.—Dr. De Forrest.—A girls' school.—Demand for educated wives.......... 186

LETTER XVI.

Constantinople.—Foreign relations of Turkey.—Arrival of Lord Stratford.—Feebleness of the Turkish government.—Corruption and public plunder.—Banditti at Smyrna.—Their robberies.—Their cruelties.—The Chiefs of the Banditti.—A Druse robber caught and caged.—The Druse population.—The Sultan.—His palace.—His Pashas.—Turkey held together by pressure without.. 202

LETTER XVII.

Beautiful view from the hill of Bulgoulu, near Constantinople.—Athens.—Corfu.—Glorious view from the Goruno.—Noble remains of ancient architecture at Athens.—Modern Greeks.—Their schools.—Their readiness to learn.—Syra.—The American consul.—Evangelides.—Dr. Hill's school.—Young ladies reading Homer in the original.—Dr. Jonas King, the orientalist.—His controversy.—His courage.—Anecdote of the American flag.—General dissatisfaction with the Greek government.—Corruption of public men 215

LETTER XVIII.

May at Rome.—Abundance of flowers.—Severity of the Roman government.—The people kept quiet by the military.—Improved appearance of Rome.—The city beautified.—Copies of old pictures.—American artists at Rome.—Sculptors.—Painters.—Gibson's Venus.—Colored statues.—Powers at Florence.—The monument of Titian at Venice....... 231

LETTER XIX.

Fresnel lights.—Their strength and brilliancy.—Improvement in their construction.—Tomb of Napoleon.—Its magnificence.—Imperfect civilization of mankind.—Exhibition of the works of living artists.—Naked Venuses.—Ugly head of Louis Napoleon.—Duveau.—Death of Agrippina 243

LETTER I.

Contraband books.—Strictness of the Custom-house Officers.—Captain Lynch and his book.—Poetry in the Custom-house.—England deluged with rain.—Prosperity of England in 1852.—Emigration to Australia.

LONDON, November 29th, 1852.

I DID not think of writing to you from England, but there are one or two things which occur to me as worthy of mention.

One of the vexations which a traveller meets on his arrival in this country is the search for contraband books. The booksellers in England have furnished the Custom-houses with a list of American works of which they claim the copyright. When a book is found among the baggage of the traveller, which is carefully overhauled for the purpose, the examining officer looks to see if it is printed in America; and if it be, he consults his manuscript list, to see whether it be also published in England by a person claiming the copyright. If its title appears on the list, the book is seized. Considerable delay is occasioned by the strictness with which the examination is made.

Among my fellow-passengers who left New York in the steamer Arctic, was Captain Lynch, the enterprising and successful explorer of the Dead Sea. He made, as you know, an official report of his expedition to the government, which has been printed by order of Congress. Besides this, he prepared a personal narrative of his expedition, a very interesting work, which was published at Philadelphia by Lea & Blanchard. Bentley, the London publisher, imported into England a number of copies of the work in sheets, procuring them to be bound; and to secure himself from competition, took out a copyright for the work, and sent the title to the Liverpool Custom-house, that any other copies introduced from America might be seized and stopped.

When Captain Lynch's baggage was undergoing examination, he asked the officer what disposition would be made of a copy of his narrative printed in America, if it was found among its effects. "Most certainly," answered the officer, "it would be my duty to retain it. Not a single work patented in this country can be introduced from abroad, and I should be obliged to seize it, even in the hands of its author."

One of our passengers had, in his portmanteau, three works published in the United States, of two of which he was the author, and to the third of which he was a contributor. One of them, a volume of poetry, required no long examination; poetry is a drug in both countries, and the publishers do not find it worth their while to mantain a very fierce rivalry for so unsalable a commodity. The volume which next engaged the officer's attention was a prose work, and this led to a long and close examination. The officer went over the list, apparently more than once, looking at the title of the book again and again, and once or twice appeared to hesitate, while the assistant inspectors stood unemployed, waiting his decision. At length he handed back the book. The third volume, a recent publication of Putnam's, was also subjected to a close scrutiny, which was, however, soon brought to a close.

On my way to this city, it seemed to me that I had never seen a country drenched like England. Seven weeks of almost constant rain have saturated the ground with water, swollen the springs, turned the ditches into streams, and raised the rivers till they have in many places swept away their bridges, and everywhere drowned the low grounds. Such numbers of wet women and children I never saw before; wet wagoners walking by the side of their dripping teams; wet laborers, male and female, digging turnips in the muddy fields; wet beggars in the towns, their rags streaming with water; wet sheep staggering under their drenched fleeces, nibbling the grass in the yellowish-green fields—for the pastures wear, at this season, a sallow verdure—or biting the turnips scattered for them by the farmers in long rows. I saw, frequently, mills standing, with their motionless wheels deep in turbid currents of water; fields prepared for grain, which cannot be sown, and others ready for the plough which cannot be ploughed. In some places, houses and even hamlets have been carried away and the inhabitants drowned; and drowned cattle, I am told, are seen floating in the currents. It is said that the country has not seen such floods since the year 1795.

Almost everybody in England speaks of the present condition of the country as extremely prosperous. The partisans of free trade insist that there has been a gradual diminution of pauperism, and an improvement in the condition of the working-classes ever since the repeal of the corn-laws. At present it is admitted that this effect has been greatly heightened by the emigration to Australia and the United States. "We have sent out," said an intelligent gentleman to me, "great numbers of laborers to Australia, the very men by whom our soil was tilled last year; the paupers, having succeeded to those places, receive the same and even better wages, and are paupers no longer. Besides these, we have sent out from other classes, particularly from the class of merchants, numbers of intelligent, enterprising men, some of the best men of England; and next year we shall give Australia a still larger host of colonists. They have gone out for a purpose of which they themselves are scarcely aware; they have gone out to found the structure of that new community on solid and liberal foundations. Within thirty years you will see a populous, prosperous, powerful, and enlightened community in Australia; and long before that time it will be independent of the mother country, for the men who have migrated to that country will not endure that it should remain in a state of dependence on a distant government a moment beyond the time when dependence is a necessity, or at least a convenience."

In the mean time I hear a good deal said of the difficulty of procuring workmen for the ordinary tasks of agriculture. During the season which has just closed, the ordinary dependence upon laborers from Ireland failed; and when the grain was to be cut, the soldiery, in order to save the crops from destruction, were sent into the fields with sickles in their hands, instead of muskets and swords. Many kinds of work, which were formerly cheaply executed, are now neglected; the more necessary employments are filled, and the others are postponed. I hear a great deal said of the depopulation of Ireland. "Ireland," said a gentleman to me, "is already half Protestant;" but this is, doubtless, an exaggeration. It is true, however, I believe, that English proprietors and farmers are going over in some numbers, and I heard of one case of an emigrant to America, who returned because he could buy land in Ireland of the same quality and nearness to the market, cheaper than in the United States.

LETTER II.

Return of gayety and commercial activity in Paris.—The *Credit Mobilier*.—The Empire succeeding a Republic which has lost its liberties. The new Emperor conducted to the Tuileries.—Absence of enthusiasm in the people.—Motives of those who voted for the Empire.—Acquiescence of all parties in the Empire.—Huntington the artist.

PARIS, December 7th, 1852.

THREE years ago, when I was in Paris, the country was suffering under that breaking up of regular employments which necessarily attends a revolution. Nobody seemed sure that another revolution, or at least an attempt at a revolution, was not close at hand; the greater part of those foreigners who make Paris their residence had flown the place. I missed the usual bustle of the streets, and saw here and there long rows of shops untenanted, with the shutters closed. At present these shops are again open, glittering with showy wares, and thronged with customers; the city is full of foreigners,—they count two thousand Americans, birds of every feather,—and the concourse of English visitors and residents seems more numerous than ever; solid English carriages rumble along the streets, and the English signs over the shop-doors seem to me nearly twice as frequent as I ever saw them before. The gayeties of the place, never extinct, are pursued with new spirit; the theatres, the public ball-rooms, and other places of entertainment, are crowded. A vehement desire of magnificence has seized upon the government; the public buildings are beautified and enlarged; workmen are busy in places, scraping from them the mould which, in this damp climate, darkens the cream-colored stone of which they are built: and all the ancient churches are undergoing extensive repairs and restorations. Old frescoes discovered on their walls under the whitewash of centuries, have been cleaned, retouched, and brightened; and eminent artists have been employed on new designs. Couture, for example, who is placed by his disciples at the head of modern French painters, is engaged on new frescoes for the church of St. Eustache. The *rue de Rivoli*, which faces the gardens of the Tuileries, is to be extended so as to traverse the entire city; a track of ruins has been opened to the west for its passage, where houses have been levelled. The magnificent parallelogram of the Louvre is to be completed, and workmen are pulling down a part of the structure not consistent with the grander plan now contemplated. Everybody is employed, and Paris, and as I am told, the whole of France, now presents an appearance of great material prosperity.

To stimulate the activity of trade the Emperor has projected a great financial scheme, a bank with an enormous capital, to be enlarged according to circumstances and the demands of borrowers, which is to lend money on mortgages of property in the country. In this way, to use an expression which I once heard from the lips of an eminent speculator in the United States, real estate is to be made fluid,—a process as much for the welfare of the body politic as it would be healthful for the human body if its solid parts were converted into a liquid state. This plan, which is to be immediately carried into effect, will stimulate speculation to a degree of which France has had no experience since the time of John Law and the South Sea bubble.

In the midst of the general activity and consequent contentment of the laboring-classes, France ceases to be a republic and becomes an empire. "I prefer the empire," said an intelligent lady to me the day after it was proclaimed, "because it is just what it pretends to be; when liberty is at end it is time that the forms of liberty should be abandoned." It was the evening before the proclamation of the empire that I arrived in Paris. The next morning the town was waked by the firing of cannon, and as the day wore on, the shops were shut, and notwithstanding the rain, for it was one of the gloomiest and saddest days of a Parisian winter, the population flocked to the Boulevards and the broader streets where detachments of the army and of the national guards were marching to the sound of music. I was present as the newly proclaimed emperor was conducted to the palace of the Tuileries by a military escort. The ceremony was rather imposing. A party of cavalry, in plumed and glittering casques, first dashed briskly forward through the space opened for them in the immense multitude which thronged the Champs Elysées and the garden of the Tuileries, like the gust which sweeps the streets before a tempest. Then came the Emperor, on horseback, amidst his generals and marshals. A few cries of *Vive l'Empereur* arose, which he answered by taking off his hat and bowing to the people. He appeared of shorter stature than most of the officers of his suite, but he sat his horse well, a spirited creature, which pranced and curvetted, and seemed proud of bearing the sovereign of the French Empire. The party entered the palace gates, and not long afterward the emperor showed himself at the balcony. The troops in front of the palace greeted his appearance with acclamations, but from the crowd which stood around me, not a single cry was heard. They were persons of all conditions and ages; well-dressed men and ladies, men in blouses and women in caps, all looking on in silence, as on a spectacle in which they had no part. There was an utter absence not only of enthusiasm but even of the least affectation of enthusiasm.

The city was illuminated in the evening—meagerly illuminated, except in a few instances. The illumination was a part of the prescribed ceremonies of the occasion, and was commanded by the government. Twice in the course of the day a message from the police was brought to the hotel where I lodge, intimating that it was expected that the house would be illuminated in the evening. The order was obeyed, of course.

It is admitted, however, I believe on all hands, that a large, at least a considerable majority of the people of France is in favor of the present order of things. At the hotel where I passed the night in Boulogne, I asked one of the attendants, a man of mature age and not unintelligent, what he thought of the empire. "What the people now want," he replied, "is the opportunity of earning their livelihood by their labor in peace. That they now have, and they are not ambitious of anything beyond it. I gave my voice for Louis Napoleon and his plans, because I believe he can and will maintain things in their present state." Another man, of nearly the same class in France, answered the same question thus: "As long as Louis Napoleon remains at peace with other nations, we shall have good times, and the people will be with him. If he should get us into a war, he will disappoint the people, and we may have another change of government.".

I was in conversation the other day with an intelligent and reflecting Frenchman, no friend of the present order of things, who said: "The character of the French race is unstable; they are swayed to and fro by the impulse of the day. A little while since they shouted *Vive la République;* now the same voices raise the cry of *Vive l'Empereur;* what may be the next cry I cannot tell; but, if we are to judge by the past, the empire of Napoleon the Third cannot last long. I do not see any elements of duration in it which did not belong to the government of Charles X. or Louis Philippe. Each of the governments which has risen and fallen since the time of Louis XVI. has promised itself eternal duration. I am waiting to see what will come next."

I give these conversations because they are more instructive than any speculations of mine would be. On Sunday I attended worship in the *Oratoire*, a French Protestant church, where I listened to an exhortation from the preacher of the day, M. Vermeuil, who dwelt on the duty of a quiet and peaceable demeanor, and admonished his hearers with much earnestness to "possess their souls in patience,"—evidently, as it seemed to me, alluding to the political circumstances of the time. Enough of French politics.

Huntington, the artist, is here, settled for the

winter. He is painting a picture of the Good Samaritan, bringing to the view the man who had fallen among thieves. He has made the studies for it with great care, and it promises to be one of his best and most interesting works.

LETTER III.

Nismes, its Roman remains, Amphitheatre, Maison Carrée and Pont du Gard.—Amphitheatre at Arles.—The Boulevards.—Roman baths.—Public garden.—Dryness of the climate.—The fountain of the Esplanade.—Delaroche's picture of Cromwell contemplating Charles I. in his coffin.

MARSEILLES, December 14th, 1852.

To those who find themselves in France and have not the time to make a journey to Rome, I would recommend a visit to Nismes. In that city and its neighborhood they will be able to obtain almost as good an idea of the remains of ancient Roman architecture as they could at Rome itself. The amphitheatre would entirely represent the Colosseum, if we were to suppose it somewhat more extensive, and somewhat more magnificent in its external architecture. The *Maison Carrée*, or Square House, a building of the Corinthian architecture, is one of the finest remains of antiquity in the world, and gives as perfect an idea as one can well have of the public edifices of the Romans. Besides these, there are the ruins of the Temple of Diana; the Gate of Augustus, a sample of their city gates; the

Grand Tower, a fragment of what was probably an immense mausoleum, and the Pont du Gard, a magnificent portion of an aqueduct which once conveyed water to the city. Not far from Nismes is the city of Arles, where is another amphitheatre and other interesting remains; and at nearly the same distance, in another direction, is Orange, with its triumphal arch in almost as good preservation as either of the triumphal arches at Rome. The monuments of antiquity at Nismes have been cleared of all encumbering rubbish, and of all the buildings erected within or against them in the course of centuries, and are thus seen to the very best advantage.

Modern Nismes is a very beautiful city. By the side of its *boulevards*, at the foot of the Temple of Diana, a vast spring, ninety feet in depth, pours forth a river of transparent water. Near it we find some remains of Roman baths, and these have been restored according to what was supposed to be their original plan, with recesses and columns, and a broad stone floor, over which the water hurries toward the town. They are overlooked by groups of statues, and protected by a massive stone balustrade. Beyond this the water is received into broad canals, bordered by walls and parapets of hewn stone, which convey it in different directions through an extensive promenade planted with trees. At the extremity of one of these, it is received into a broad circular basin of stone, the sides of which slope by an easy descent, and here the washerwomen of Nismes ply their vocation, slapping and rubbing the wet linen, and make the slow current froth with soap. On the rocky hill which rises above the fountain a public garden has been laid out. The bare cliffs, about the middle of the last century, were covered with soil brought up from the plain, intersected with winding walks and planted thickly with pines and cypresses, among which are thickets of laurels, myrtle, the tree-box, the lauratinus, with its clusters of white flowers, now beginning to open, and a variety of other shrubs and trees which never drop their leaves in the season of winter. You might walk here in one of the sunny winter days of this soft climate and fancy it to be May. Above the garden on its foundation of rock rises the lofty Roman ruin, the Grand Tower.

Those parts of the town which lie near these

public grounds have an uncommonly agreeable aspect. The streets are very broad and the houses are in a pleasing style of architecture, built of the cream-colored stone of the country, which is easily wrought, and which in the dry climate of this place long retains its original rich light tint in the open air. It appears to me that the aridity of the climate has much to do with the preservation of the ancient buildings. At Lyons and Avignon, on the Rhone, the exhalations from the river darken the churches and houses almost to a sooty hue, and here at Marseilles on the Mediterranean, I perceive the same effect. The frescoes of Deveria, in the Cathedral at Avignon, painted twelve years since, and well worthy of a longer date, are already peeling in flakes from the walls and the ceiling, so damp is the atmosphere there. Nismes is situated on a plain elevated considerably above the meadows of the Rhone, and beyond the reach of its mists. I was told that rain is sometimes known not to fall in this region for ten months together. I inquired what, in that case, became of the crops. "They are gathered early," was the answer, "except our principal harvests, grapes and olives, and these are best in a dry climate. We have our last showers in April, and then we expect no more rain till October." In such an atmosphere moss and mould are slow in gathering upon walls and sculptures in the open air, and the oldest remains of these at Nismes, such, for example, as the rich Corinthian columns of the *Maison Carrée*, only acquire a warm brown tint after the lapse of centuries.

One of the modern ornaments of Nismes is the Fountain of the Esplanade, adorning the principal public square, a work of the French sculptor Pradier, who died about six months since by a stroke of apoplexy. It is a group representing Nismes with a crown of towers and palaces, copied from the Roman remains, and the streams which water the neighboring lands sitting at her feet, among which is the little river gushing from the ground in the public garden, a beautiful female figure just emerging from girlhood, her fair brows shaded with a chaplet of the leaves of the water-lily. It is a work of considerable merit, but there is a finer one of the same artist in the cathedral at Avignon, a Virgin of great beauty of form and an ethereal sweetness of expression.

The *Maison Carrée* is turned into a Museum, that is to say, into a public gallery of pictures. It has some fine portraits by Vanloo, several good cabinet pictures of the Flemish school, and a few larger ones by French painters; but the most striking of them all, as it seemed to me, was Delaroche's painting of Cromwell contemplating the dead body of Charles the First in its coffin. Delaroche is among painters what Crabbe is among poets; he confines himself to rugged, unidealized nature. One would hardly suppose it possible for a French artist to renounce so completely, not only all that is theatrical in the French school, but all attempt at grace of any sort, as he has done in this work. As I looked at the rough old Roundhead uncovering, with that sad expression which speaks so much of the feelings within, the lifeless face of his king, I could not help fancying myself with him in the chamber of death.

It is impossible for me here in the south of France, to help imagining myself in Italy. The mild climate, the vast tracts covered with olive-trees and intermingled vineyards, the Italian character of the architecture, the women drawing water from the fountains in jars of antique form, the people showing in their features and physiognomy a certain kindred to the Italian race, and speaking an accented language bequeathed to them by the troubadours, almost as different from the language of the northern provinces as that of Spain or Portugal, make it hard for me to convince myself that I am still within the boundaries of France. Around me are the descendants of Roman and Greek colonists, who have founded prosperous and flourishing communities; of those who came hither when the family of Constantine fixed the seat of the Roman empire at Arles, and of those of a later age, when the Italian church migrated, for a time, to Avignon, and made it an Italian city.

To judge by appearances, this part of the population of France, as well as that of the north, is as perfectly satisfied with the present government as if they had lived under an empire from the days of Constantine. No external indication, certainly, bespeaks discontent; there is nothing of gravity or of gloom—no silence, sulkiness, or sadness. It is characteristic of the French race, that it conforms itself easily to any change of circumstances, provided you do not interfere with its amusements. "What a people!" said a German lady to me at Paris. "Three or four thousand unoffending and unresisting people—men, women, and children—were shot in the streets, at their doors, at their windows, or sitting in their apartments, a year ago, when Louis Napoleon abolished the French constitution. In a few weeks all recollection of the dreadful event seemed to have passed away. What a people, that such things should have been done, and that, after a few days, nothing should be said of them; that they should have been forgotten and pardoned!"

Yet there are some who speculate on political events in this country, and who occupy themselves in working out the problem by what sort of process the present government will by and by follow its predecessors to the place where they are all to sleep together. One of them lately said to me: "The Emperor is surrounded by able men, very able and wholly unprincipled, whose advice and assistance he has had in the well-managed intrigue which has made him the absolute sovereign of France. Hitherto, while the project was yet unconsummated, they all acted harmoniously together, for they had but one object. Now the time has arrived for rewarding their services with honors and emoluments, and from this time each will have a particular aim of his own; each will claim the highest reward for himself. It will be impossible for the Emperor to satisfy them. It is not that they will be discontented with what they receive, but that they will be indignant to see others placed over them. Then will be the time of feuds and factions, which as yet under the new order of things have been unknown; then will secret intrigues be set on foot to excite discontent against the government, which, after being adroitly kindled and inflamed for a few years, may unseat Louis Napoleon as easily as it unseated Charles the Tenth or Louis Philippe!"

There may be much truth in this view, but it seems to me that one of the greatest dangers which the new Emperor has to dread will arise from another cause. In the circumstances in which he has hitherto been placed, audacity has been the highest policy. He is now about to apply the same policy to measures of finance, in which it is madness. Everything indicates that the reign of speculation has begun in France, under the auspices of the new bank, established to increase the number of borrowers to an extent hitherto unknown in the country. The unhealthy prosperity of a period of speculation will be followed most certainly by a period of embarrassment, bankruptcy, and the want of employment among the working-classes. Man, like all beasts of prey, is fierce when famished. A hungry Frenchman has something in him of the nature of the wolves which in a severe winter descend from the mountains of his own country and attack the peasants at their doors. It was the want of employment, it was idleness and famine, which gave rise to the several attempts to change the government by violence that so soon followed the revolution of 1848.

LETTER IV.

Security from accident on board the Mediterranean steamers.—Discomforts of a small steamer.—Fine view of the Maritime Alps from the water.—A day in Genoa.—Vexations of the passport system.—Pæstum Amalfi.—Neapolitan boatmen.—Beauty of the coast.—Songs of the boatmen.—Peculiarities of Neapolitan pronunciation.—Excursion to Pæstum.—Sickly inhabitants.—Messina.—Malta.—La Valletta.—The Catholic church in Malta.

VALLETTA, ISLAND OF MALTA, Dec. 29, 1852.

AT Marseilles they told me that though there are more than fifty steamers now on the Mediterranean, not a shipwreck or disastrous accident of any kind has happened to any of them since steamers were first introduced on these waters, with the exception of a single instance, and that happened some twenty years since. They all have low-pressure engines, are carefully navigated, and the greater number of them merely make coasting voyages, stopping at one port after another,' and never putting to sea when the weather is tempestuous. It was in one of these steamers that on the 14th of this month I took passage for Naples—a little Neapolitan boat, short and broad, tumbling about with every impulse of the waves and wind, and working her way as well as might be with a weak engine. The motion, as we proceeded out of the harbor, soon drove all the passengers to their berths, except those who were proof against the causes of sea-sickness. In passing between a rocky island and the coast, our poor boat had her wheels entangled among the ropes of a net, and was an hour or more getting clear of them.

I had, some years before, travelled the road along what is called the Maritime Alps, from Marseilles to Nice, and thought the scenery extremely grand, but I am not quite sure that it is not finer when viewed from the water. You take broader views of it, at least, and see how its several parts add to each other's effect. As the mountain summits, one by one, rise before you— the loftiest, at this season, glistening with snow —as the gulfs, and bays, and valleys, and ravines, one by one, open upon you; as town after town shows itself, spread out upon the shelving shore, or nestling in the lap of hills, or seated on the craggy heights, the attention is kept ever awake with ever-new images of sublimity and beauty. A sea-voyage is a comfortless thing always, at least I have found it so—but a sea-voyage which shows such sights as these, brings some compensation for its discomfort.

In about thirty hours our steamer brought us to Genoa, where the passengers were counted like sheep, to see that their number was neither too large nor too small; and then, after an hour's delay or more, we were permitted, by the police of the place, to land, in a dark, rainy evening, and proceeded to an hotel—for these boats, while in port at any of their stopping-places, do not concern themselves with providing for their passengers. We had a day—a bright, sunny, cheerful, winter-day of Italy—to look at the palaces and churches of Genoa, and all the glorious views seen from its heights; and, leaving the place in the evening, were early the next morning at Leghorn, where the examination of the passports of those who wished to land occasioned still longer delays. We received, however, at last, permission to go on shore, and having breakfasted went by railway to Pisa, to get a hasty look at its antiquities. Another night on the water brought us to the port of Civita Vecchia, where we thought we should be starved before the police would allow us to land. At last an officer made his appearance on board with written permissions for all of us, between fifty and sixty in number; our names were called, and as we answered to them we were permitted to step down to the boats, waiting to convey us to the shore. We had just time to breakfast, see the greater number of our fellow-passengers depart on their way to Rome, and make a rapid circuit of the little town, to be convinced that it contained nothing worth seeing, when the time arrived for returning to our steamer. It had been lightened of the greater part of its cargo, and now in going out of port bobbed and danced like a cork upon the waves. After a most unpleasant passage, the early light of the fifth morning from our embarking saw us rounding the coast of Baiæ, and making our way slowly against a north wind. At half-past nine we dropped anchor, but nobody was permitted to go on shore till an hour and a half afterward, when we stepped into boats, were taken before the police authorities, and received written permission to remain in the capital of the kingdom for twenty-four hours, at the end of which we were to make application either for leave to remain still longer, or leave to depart. We got to our hotel, and breakfasted about twelve o'clock. I have been the more particular in this recital because it illustrates the beauty of the passport system, and shows what a pleasant thing it is for the traveller. In France, since the late revolution, this system has been somewhat modified, and made more tolerable, but in the other countries of Europe it prevails at the present moment in its worst rigor. The other day a party of dragoons came on board one of the steamers touching at Messina, and took the English passengers before the police, where they underwent an examination.

During our stay at Naples we made an excursion to Pæstum, of which, however, I should not have said much, were it not for the episode of a visit to Amalfi on our way—a place remarkable for the exceeding beauty of its scenery.

We left Naples by the earliest railway train for Nocera, a little town ten miles, perhaps, beyond Pompeii. It had been a cold night for Naples; the tramontane winds had been blowing for two days, a calm still night had succeeded, and the hoar-frost was now glistening by the side of the way. As we dismounted to take a look at

Pompeii in passing, I found by touching the earth with the end of my umbrella that the frost had hardened to thin crust on the surface of the soil, though the fields of lupines and broad-beans around us, already half grown, seemed uninjured by it. This was a Neapolitan winter in its greatest severity. Our cicerone, after a few minutes' flourish with his hands, would stop to rub them vehemently, and complain of the cold. As the sun mounted the day became warm and genial. We returned to the railway, reached Nocera in a few minutes, and made a bargain with the most respectable looking of the carriage-drivers who crowded shouting around us, to convey us to Salerno.

We passed up among the mountains, through a beautiful and fertile valley, among vineyards and plantations of the fig-tree and rows of olive-trees, and crops of every green thing the season could produce, except grass—but let no one look for grass in Southern Italy. Every spot of earth which will bear tillage is furrowed with the plough and turned with the spade, and the only places where grass is allowed to spring up are the borders of the road and the narrow edges of the fields. Of course you never see any broad expanse of greensward, such as with us is so fresh and grateful to the eye, and forms so pleasant a carpet for the feet, unless in those tracts from which the cultivator is driven by the malaria.

After a drive of four or five miles, we began to descend toward the sea-shore. We had left on our right the grand mountain promontory on which stand the towns of Sorrento and Castellamare, and now the broad gulf of Salerno lay before us, embraced by a semicircle of lofty mountains. Far to the southeast, on a level between the base and the sea, our driver pointed out to us the site of Pæstum. About midday we were at Salerno, a city of twenty thousand inhabitants, dirty and noisy, and full of beggars, with olive groves on the rocky slopes back of it, and the finest orange orchards along the shore which I have seen in Italy, loaded and bending with their yellow but not fully ripened fruit. It was now too late, they told us, to think of going to Pæstum and returning the same day; we therefore engaged a boat to take us to Amalfi.

It was a clumsy thing, manned with four rowers, each of whom, standing upright, pushed instead of pulling a huge oar, held to a pin in the edge of the boat by a thong, or piece of rope. The principal among them was a merry fellow from Amalfi, about five feet in height, wearing a Phrygian cap, and a dress composed of a canvas shirt and drawers. He and one of his companions took us on their shoulders, and carried us through the shallow water to the boat. As the oarsmen struck out into the bay, he pulled off his cap, threw it on the seat, and encouraged them by calling out, "*Allez*, pull away, pull away, ugh." The boatmen in this part of the Mediterranean appear to have adopted the words "pull away" from the English sailors, for I heard them using it again at Messina. At every repetition of "*Allez*, pull away, pull away, ugh," the boatmen would lean to their oars and redouble the strokes.

As we passed along beside the rocks which rise out of the transparent water of the Mediterranean, we were struck with the wonderful beauty of the region.

"Earth has not anything to show more fair."

In the recesses of the mountains, close to the

sea, nestled the white villages of the fishermen, the dwellings of those who tend the olive-tree and the vine were clustered on the heights; the midway declivities were clothed with the gray-green of olive groves, with thickets of the prickly pear hanging from the cliffs in masses of uncouth vegetation; higher up grew trees of deeper verdure, the corob, which bears a sort of bean, imbedded in a sweet pulp, the food of horses; and above them all, bare pinnacles of rock rose into the clear blue sky. Here and there we descried a convent, perched far up in a spot that seemed inaccessible; and on the precipices by the sea rose old towers, built to protect the country from the invasions of the Saracens, and long since abandoned. The whole scene was bathed in a mild golden sunshine, and the smooth waves rippled softly on the beaches, or rolled with gentle dashes into the caverns of the rocks. Our boatmen sang as they rowed, keeping time to the stroke of their oars. Their songs were sometimes plaintive and sometimes comic, but as they were in the Neapolitan dialect, I could not make out their meaning. Our courier, however, who was four years and a half dragoman to the Grand

Turk at Constantinople, and who, besides Turkish, Arabic, and modern Greek, understands all the dialects of Italy, explained them to us, and made, what I dare say was sprightly enough in the original, very tedious in the interpretation. Besides other peculiarities, which are numerous enough, the people of the Neapolitan dominions have an odd way of pronouncing Italian, which may be exemplified in English thus:

"Faindly as dolls the evening gime
Our voices geep dune and our oars geep dime."

And again,

"The rabids are near and the daylighd's bast."

Just before arriving at Amalfi, we passed the village of Atrani, seated in a steep and narrow gorge, where a little stream comes down from the mountains, and high up among the precipices a small white house was pointed out, by our merry friend the boatman, as the house of Masaniello, the fisherman who became a politician and a revolutionist. "And who was Masaniello?" I asked.

"He was a great king of the country," answered the boatman.

This is all that the large majority of Masaniello's countrymen know about him. The patriot and republican is confounded by the people with the common rabble of dead kings.

As we approached Amalfi, our little boatman raising his cry of "*Allez*, pull away, pull away, ugh," looked over his shoulder at us, nodded and smiled, and our boat was soon upon the beach, where a crowd of swarthy fellows, in woollen caps and tattered pantaloons, were waiting to carry us to the shore on their shoulders; and as soon as our boat touched the sand, they gathered round it, up to their knees in the water, thrusting each other aside, and all shouting at once. We tried to select the best only for our bearers, and when at length we landed, the whole crowd ran after us, every man of them, as it seemed to me, demanding to be paid. Our train was further re-enforced by the beggars, blind and lame, who always haunt the places where strangers are expected to pass. We obtained a guide, looked at the old cathedral, which contains little of interest, and then proceeded to what is called the Valley of the Mills, a deep ravine between precipices of immense height at the mouth of which this little town of seven thousand inhabitants is built. A stream—a brook rather—rushes along at the bottom, and turns seventeen paper-mills. Orange-trees, loaded with fruit, overhang the path from the walls of narrow gardens, and other fruit-trees of various kinds, not now in leaf, and trailing plants in full verdure, nourished by the perpetual moisture, mantle the rocks with their luxuriant growth. High above rise the crags, crowned with old dwellings, castles, and convents; and, seaward, through the chasm, you have a glimpse of Salerno, and the mountains of the opposite coast. It is a spot for the pencil, and not for description.

We climbed to the Franciscan convent overlooking the shore, and from a natural grotto extending deep into the rock, had a magnificent view of the shore, the sea, and the distant mountains. Part of the nearer crags were lying in shadow, yet distinct, a sort of clear-obscure, and part were crimson with the descending sun. We returned to Salerno by moonlight, our boatmen singing the popular ballads of the country, as they passed under the rocks of the shore.

We set out the next morning for Pæstum at

half-past four. For miles beyond Salerno, we found the road, at that hour, full of men and women trooping to the town, with donkeys bearing loads of vegetables and roots, and wagons and carts drawn by white oxen, loaded with wine, grain, and pulse, the productions of the country. Herds of swine were driven by us, squealing as they went, and several flocks of sheep. If early rising be a sign of industry, the people of this part of Italy well deserve to be called industrious. We could perceive that we were passing through a highly cultivated region, though with but few inhabitants; but when at length the daylight came we found ourselves travelling alone in a solitary level tract of pasturage, spotted with luxuriant tufts of thistles, in which herds of white cows and black buffaloes were grazing. To our left were the mountains with villages and towns on their sides, and the sea was moaning on our right. Further on, tracts of springing wheat made their appearance, fields of turnips and lupines luxuriantly green, with here and there a building apparently intended as a storehouse for the crops.

"There is Pæstum," said one of our party.

Looking before us, we saw at a little distance the majestic columns of the temple of Ceres, and in a few minutes passed through the opening made by the road in the ruined walls of the ancient town, and stopped at the door of a house which answered, in some respects, the purpose of a hostelry. We found a *cicerone*, who carried a bunch of keys and opened for us the iron gate of the enclosure in which the Temple of Ceres stands. I will not repeat for you what is said in the guide-books of these fine remains of Greek architecture. The Temple of Neptune, as it is the most ancient, is the noblest and most imposing in aspect. It is wonderful how this atmosphere, in which man sickens and dies, spares the work of his hands. In many parts, the architectural ornaments of the Temple of Neptune are as perfect and as sharp in outline as if they were cut yesterday, and nowhere is the stone incrusted with moss, or darkened with mould; time has only given it a warmer tint. The ground, within their grand colonnades, was spotted with December daisies, in bloom, and the morning air was scented with the sweet alyssum, which grows here in profusion, its white flowers, at that time, looking at a little distance like hoar-frost. I was surprised to see so much cultivation; the fields were enclosed with stone walls and rude hedges; there was a vineyard near, and plantations of fig-trees; and wheat had been sown and was just springing up, close to the foundation-stones of the Temple of Ceres. Nor was the place so solitary as I expected to find it. Travellers were passing to and fro on the highway by which we came; a diligence full of passengers went by; a party of sportsmen, with their fowling-pieces, stopped at the inn; we saw several soldiers in uniform in the road, and when we were not within the enclosures containing the temples, we had a train of followers, some of whom wanted to sell us old coins, which they pretended to have found, and others importuned us for alms.

I asked our guide if the soil of the place was productive. "By no means," he replied; "the earth is full of salt, and there are no springs; in summer these fields are scorched by a severe drought. Those who cultivate them live at Carpaccio, yonder, where there is good air and good water." Here he pointed to a village in sight, half-way up the mountain-side. "In summer," he continued, "this place is so unhealthy that nobody dares to sleep here; those who look to the crops come down in the daytime, and return before night-fall. It swarms with snakes, too, which in summer crawl out of the old walls, and are very dangerous. There are some of the people who remain here during the summer."

As he said this, he pointed to a group of half a dozen people, none of whom seemed to have reached the middle term of life, emaciated, pale, and ragged, most of them wearing a look of helpless debility. We were then about entering our carriage, to take the luncheon which we had brought with us. One of our party threw on the ground the thigh-bone of a chicken, which had been well picked. A boy stepped from the sickly group, took it up, examined it narrowly, and finding it perfectly bare, threw it back again. It was evident that the poor creatures were hungry. We made a pretty liberal distribution of bread and cheese, and bits of meat, among the ghastly women and pallid children, and drove off for Salerno, from which we proceeded to Nocera, and reached Naples by the last train for the day.

To the island of Malta we came by a French steamer—the Hellespont, plying between Marseilles and Alexandria, a more powerful and commodious boat than the Maria Antoinetta. We shot over smooth water by the now harmless rock of Scylla, with a little town behind it on the Calabrian coast, and ran close by the inoffensive eddy of Charybdis, near a village of fishermen on the Sicilian side. "They make a great deal of Scylla and Charybdis in romances," said the second captain of our steamer, "but they are nothing." Of Messina, where we touched, and remained for two or three hours, I have only one remark to make—that the people, though slight and short of stature, have incredibly powerful voices; they are noisier than even the Neapolitans. We passed through the market-place, where they were screaming their wares at the highest pitch of their voices, and I think I was never in so deafening an uproar. In about forty-two hours from the time of leaving Naples we were in the port of Valletta, the principal city of Malta.

To a New Yorker it is worth a voyage across the Atlantic to see so clean a city as Valletta. It is admirably well built, of a cream-colored calcareous rock, which they hew with axes, and shape with ease into any form that suits the architect. The streets are paved with the same material, which is almost as little soiled under the feet of passengers, as the walls of the houses themselves. Seaward and landward the town is protected by fortification beyond fortification, rampart beyond rampart, and several of its gates are cut through the living rock. From the ramparts, or from the flat housetops of the town, you have a view of the interior of the island, which presents a very uninviting aspect. High walls of stone divide it into little enclosures, where the rock is covered with soil, brought, for the most part, it is said, from Sicily. At first sight one would say that there are no trees on the island, but on looking more closely, you perceive rows of sprawling fig-trees planted by the walls, their boughs given off close to the ground, and here and there a corob-tree, an evergreen, larger but equally sprawling. All the trees on this island, except those which grow in the lower and moister situations, have this tendency to put out their branches close to the earth, and to creep rather than to rise.

Whether it be the effect of the sea-winds which sweep over the island from every point of the compass, or of the want of depth of soil, I do not profess to decide.

Just now a question of local politics has arisen in the island, which is not without general interest. When the English took possession of the Island of Malta, they engaged to maintain the Roman Catholic church in all its existing rights. This does not seem to have been understood to imply that other modes of worship were not to be tolerated, and, accordingly, other denominations of Christians have established their worship here. When, however, some years since, the Methodists built a church in Valletta, they were prohibited from giving it any of the external indications of a place for public devotions. Since that time, and within a few years, a very fine building, in which the service of the Anglican church is performed, has been erected: the most conspicuous in appearance of all the churches in Valletta. This seems to have given some displeasure to the Catholic priesthood, and to the original Maltese population, who, to a man, are devout Catholics.

A new criminal code has lately been drawn up for the island; a code very judiciously framed, in general, as I am told, and to which it is very desirable that validity should be given as early as possible. It has, however, been the subject of long debate and consideration in the Council of the island. Malta you know is ruled by a governor and a council the members of which are partly appointed by the home government, and partly elected by the people. In one of the articles providing punishment for the disturbance of public worship, the Roman Catholic church is styled the dominant church of the country. This expression, after a vehement struggle on the part of the Catholics to retain it, has just been struck out of the code. Those who desired to retain it argued with some plausibility that the British government found the Roman Catholic church dominant in Malta, and by promising to maintain it in the exercise of its rights, had engaged to keep it so. Those who insisted on striking out the expression, took the higher ground of liberty of conscience, and argued that under a just government all forms of religion should be placed on a footing of equality in the eye of the law.

The archbishop of Malta has written a letter to the governor of the island, protesting against the omission of the epithet "dominant," as applied to the church of which he is a dignitary, and declaring that if the word is not restored, he and his clergy will petition the home government for its restoration. The governor has answered that there is no probability that the home government will grant the petition. The petition has probably by this time been forwarded.

To-morrow we shall probably leave this place in an English steamer for Egypt.

LETTER V.

Voyage from Malta to Cairo.—A steamer crowded with passengers from England to India.—Ill-bred people.—Fortune, the botanist.—The tea-plant in America and India.—The grape in China and Japan.—A Chinese fruit for America.—A hardy palm.—Arrival at Alexandria.—Confusion of the landing.—Passage to Cairo.—The canal.—the Nile.—Arab devotions.—Youth drowned in the Nile.

CAIRO, EGYPT, January 12th, 1853.

I LEFT Malta on the 30th December in the British steamer Ripon, proceeding to Alexandria in one of her monthly voyages from Southampton. Her commander was Captain Moresby, a veteran in the British naval service, known to geographers by his chart of the Red Sea and the Maldive Islands. We found a crowd of English on board on their way to India, army-officers, civilians, medical men, a score of ladies, a lord or two, the Governor of Hong Kong, a Chief Justice of the India bench, and a large number of cadets, some of them scarcely full grown, sent out to fill the civil and military employments, which are kept for young men who must be provided for.

"These youths," said a Major in the British service, who had been my fellow-passenger on board of the Arctic, and whom I was very glad to meet again, " will find, in the climate of India, a severe trial for their constitutions; and yet it is necessary that they should go out thus early, in order to qualify them properly for the posts they are to hold. A great many of them will die, and leave their places vacant for other adventurers." I looked at their fresh and healthy countenances, as he said this, and wished them well through the trial; but a fate was hanging over one of them more sudden and disastrous than any of us could possibly anticipate.

The cabins in the Ripon, called with us state-rooms, contain each generally four berths, and when occupied by more than two persons, are particularly inconvenient. As we found no one of them vacant, our party was billeted in different chambers, among persons who doubtless wished us back to America with all their hearts. The proportion of ill-bred people on board was greater than I expected to find. Passengers, late at night, would come singing to their berths, or whistle perseveringly as they turned over and arranged the contents of their portmanteaus, or bore you with their elbows, and commit various other acts of petty rudeness. One day—it was the first of January—the captain gave champagne at dinner, and immediately a strife arose among about a third part of the passengers, as it seemed to me, to see who should get possession of the bottles, and swallow the most of their contents. The supply was liberal, and we had a noisy night.

Among the passengers was Mr. Fortune, the botanist and traveller, who had already made two visits to China, with a view of ascertaining which of the vegetable productions of that country might be advantageously introduced into the British dominions, and was now proceeding on a third voyage to Shanghae, by way of India. I sought an acquaintance with him, which he did not decline, and I was much interested by his conversation. "You are attempting the introduction of the tea-plant into America," he said, "but I doubt whether you will succeed. Your climate, with its warm summer, is well adapted to its cultivation, and you will probably have no difficulty in finding soils suitable for its growth; but labor is so dear in the United States, and so cheap in China, that the Chinese will send it to your doors at far less cost than you can produce it at home. I am at present engaged in the experiment of introducing the tea-plant into India. On the slopes of the Himalaya mountains are a soil and climate perfectly adapted to its cultivation; a country where land can be had for almost nothing, and labor costs very little. Here we are now forming gardens of the tea-plant, and I have, for my part, no doubt of the success of the undertaking."

We talked of the culture of the grape in America. "If, as you say," said Mr. Fortune, "the European grape does not succeed well with you, I should advise you to import stocks from those varieties of it which are cultivated in China, where the climate so much resembles your own in its changes and extremes. In the northern parts of China which I visited, I found a table grape very common, though they make no wine. You might easily have the plants brought over, as you are now beginning to have a pretty extensive commerce with the ports north of Canton. We have better fruit of the kind in Europe than I saw there, but you might perhaps improve it.

"There is one kind of fruit," he continued, "which I am introducing into Northern India, and which, I am sure, would succeed in some parts of your country. It is called in China the *yang-mae*—a fruit of the size of a plum, resembling that of the arbutus, but larger—a crimson berry, covered all over with small projecting points, very agreeable to the palate, and with just acidity enough in its flavor to make it refreshing. You have in America some plants of the genus to which it belongs, the *myrica*."

I instanced the *myrica cerifera*, or candleberry myrtle, bearing large quantities of berries.

"The *yang-mae* also," proceeds Mr. Fortune, "is an abundant bearer. It will not answer for England, as our summers are not warm enough, but in those parts of the United States, where the mercury in Fahrenheit's thermometer does not fall in winter below twenty, or, at the utmost, twelve degrees, and where you have a nice warm summer"—such was his phrase—"to ripen it, the fruit would be produced in perfection. It would be well worth the while of some of your horticulturists to take measures for introducing it from the northern parts of China."

In a subsequent conversation, Mr. Fortune mentioned a hardy kind of palm, the only one which will grow in cold climates, and very common in some parts of China. "It requires," he observed, "a warm summer, and will bear a severe winter, and is the very tree for the United States. It is a *chamærops*, a genus of the palm family, of which there are several species, all of them tropical plants but this. It looks strange, in the depth of winter, to see this tree, apparently a production of the tropics, with its large evergreen leaves loaded with snow. The Chinese obtain from the upper part of it a kind of network, the sheathing of the young leaves, knotted with the most perfect regularity, which they apply to many useful purposes."

On his way to China, Mr. Fortune was taking out with him to Calcutta several cases containing cinchona plants—the tree which produces the Peruvian bark—brought from South America, with the design of introducing it into India.

As we approached Egypt, the weather grew rainy, and at length the pharos of Alexandria appeared above a low, flat shore. A pilot of slender figure, a little stooping, with a dirty white turban on his head, and a loose blue bag covering his legs from the waist to a little below the knee, came on board. Our steamer made a sudden turn, swept into the harbor, and dropped anchor in a violent shower, under fortifications bristling with guns placed in full sight. On landing we were at once surrounded by a mob of fellows in white turbans or fez caps, and blue cotton shirts tied round the waist by a string, offering us their donkeys with loud shouts, thrusting each other aside to get at us, and blocking our way so that we could not get forward a single step. As there was apparently no alternative, I took the one who stood immediately before me by the throat, shoved him out of my way, and then attacked the next in like manner, till I made my escape out of the crowd. The good-natured Mussulmans smiled at finding themselves thus unceremoniously handled by an infidel, and I jumped upon one of the best looking of their animals, and trotted off through streets swimming with white mud to the hotel, followed by a shouting donkey-driver, who brandished a long stick, which he occasionally brought down on the quadruped's flanks to encourage his speed.

Brief space was allowed us to look from our hotel windows at the strange spectacle of people in oriental costumes, men and women, walking the streets, or trotting gently by on asses, or urging forward laden camels. We had a gallop on donkeys, attended by a dragoman richly dressed for the occasion, to attract custom, and three or four donkey-drivers running on foot, to Cleopatra's Needle and Pompey's Pillar, which I will not tire you with describing. I have scarcely time to notice a spacious garden by which we passed, full of lofty date-palms and large-leaved bananas, or to observe the beauty of an avenue through which we went, planted with cassia-trees in full verdure. In a short time we were on board the boat destined to take us to the Nile, through the broad canal opened by the late pacha, Mehemet Ali. Here forty or fifty passengers, who had come by the steamer Ripon to Alexandria, passed the night, as well as they might, on benches, tables, and camp-stools. I grew tired of my hard couch, and went on deck before the day dawned. The moon, in her wane, was in the firmament, which seemed enlarged to an immense depth; and the deck, in the transparent atmosphere, was drenched with dew. A small steamer was dragging us along the canal, and at the helm of our boat stood an Egyptian, in a shaggy brown capote, motionless as a statue, with one or two in the same garb squatted on the deck near him. To the right and left nothing was to be seen but the heaps of mould formed in digging the canal.

When the day broke we found ourselves gliding on between rows of large trees in luxuriant leaf: the cassia, the thorny acacia, called by the ancients the acanthus, and the sycamore, a tree producing a kind of fig, which forms a considerable part of the food of the Egyptians. From time to time we passed villages on the bank, built of unburnt brick, with low, flat roofs, looking like the habitations of mud-wasps magnified. Each had its mosque, with a minaret of hewn stone, from which the hour of prayer is proclaimed. Their inmates, in turbans and long blue or white cotton shirts, were creeping out of them in the early sunshine, and walking carefully on the wet and slippery declivity. Among them were women in blue cotton gowns, barefooted, with infants perched on their shoulders. This is the way in which the Arab mothers, of the laboring class in Egypt, carry their children; as soon as the little creatures get the primary use of their limbs, they are transferred from the arms to the shoulders. I have seen instances of this custom which would supply striking subjects for the pencil. At Old Cairo, the other day, a Coptic woman, in the loose blue dress of the country, barefooted, her face unveiled, with dark symmetrical features, silent and sad-looking, opened to us the door of the old worm-eaten church in which is the little grotto where the Holy Virgin, with her child, is said to have eluded the pursuit of Herod. On the woman's shoulder sat an infant of seven or eight months, as silent as the mother, with well-formed brown cheeks and long dark eyelashes, its head bowed upon hers, and one little hand pressed against her forehead while the other arm was passed around the back of the neck. The Egyptian mothers treat their children with great tenderness, and though I see infants everywhere, I do not know that I have yet heard one of them cry. The expression of quiet resignation in their faces is often quite touching. The Egyptian, born to a lot of dirt, poverty, and oppression, may well learn patience early.

At eight o'clock in the morning we reached the Nile, and were transferred to a steamer. About half the passengers of the Ripon had been sent on a little before us by another. We passed a day on the Nile, and had ample opportunity to observe the character of the great river and its banks. It is a turbid stream, like the Mississippi, flowing rapidly toward the ocean, between banks of fine mould, which are easily undermined, and crumble into the current. The broad, level tracts by which it is bordered have the same dark rich soil as that which lies about our rivers of the West. Along the bank where the current has worn it away, you see distinctly the layers of mould, which, year after year, have been deposited by the successive inundations, and which attest that the land of Egypt has been gradually rising for ages. The bed of the river appears to have been raised also in an equal degree, and I have been told by those who have made the examination for themselves, that, although in some places the sands of the desert, blown by the winds, have encroached upon the fertile grounds, in others the area of fertility has been extended. Broad tracts of sand, which the waters never reached before, have been overlaid by the slime of the river, and, after one or two inundations, covered with harvests.

The country on each side of the Nile was green with tracts of clover, lentiles, barley, and other grains and pulse. Groves of the date-palm appeared by the river-side, and showed their lofty tops at a distance; here and there were seen clumps of the cassia and acanthus, or a huge branching sycamore, overshadowing the tomb of a Mahommedan saint. As the day wore on, we saw men beginning their daily toil of raising water from the river by means of a wheel turned by a donkey, and furnished with buckets, to irrigate the surrounding fields. Women, some of them carefully concealing their faces, and others leaving them exposed, came down to the stream, and filled large earthen jars with the water, which they bore off on their heads. People in turbans, carrying long pipes, were seen walking, or riding donkeys, sometimes with an attendant, or running on foot, along the causeys built to form a passage from place to place during the floods.

Our captain and his crew were Egyptians, though the engineer was an Englishman. They set us an edifying example of Mahommedan devotion. As the Mussulman prays four times a day, and not more than one of the hands could be spared from his employment at any one time, there was scarcely an hour of the day in which some one of them was not in the act of prayer. Each of them, as his turn came, mounted the right wheel-house, and made his prostrations, and murmured his devotions with closed eyes and moving lips in the presence of all the passengers.

At length, after a second uncomfortable night passed on benches and stools, we reached the landing-place of the steamer Bulak, a mile or thereabouts below Cairo. We were conveyed by omnibuses through a fine avenue of trees with dense foliage to our hotels, in the Frank quarter of the city. Here we heard of the fate of one of our fellow-passengers in the Ripon. He was a fair-haired youth, scarcely grown to his full stature, of the name of Frazer, who, with another of the same age, was going out to his father in India, leaving a mother in England. I had observed him always with his young friend, and had been interested not a little by his ingenuous physiognomy. In coming on from Alexandria to Cairo the passengers by the Ripon had been separated into two divisions, and sent on by different steamers; the one which had the young Frazer on board, preceded by three or four hours the one in which I was. In climbing some part of the rigging, the evening before our arrival, he missed his hold and fell into the river. The steamer was immediately stopped, and everything done to save him, but to no purpose. He strove to swim toward the steamer against the strong current; he breasted it gallantly for a while, but it carried him down, and he appeared no more. He sleeps with the Pharaohs and the shepherd-kings. His father and mother will hear of his death almost at the same moment; the one by the caravan of adventurers who came on with us on their way to India, and the other by the return of the Ripon to England.

LETTER VI.

Sights and sounds of Cairo.—Aspect of the crowd in the streets.—Women.—The bazars.—The barbers.—Mosques.—Noisy habits of the Egyptians.—Mosque of Mohammed Ali.—The pyramids of Ghizeh.—Arab boatmen.—Bedouins.—Purpose of the pyramids.—Pyramids of Sakkara.—M. Mariette and his excavations.—Temple and tomb of Apis.—The site of Memphis.—Mounds of sun-dried brick.—Vast grove of palms.—Saltpetre manufactured from the bricks.

CAIRO, EGYPT, January 29th, 1853.

My last letter closed with my arrival at Cairo. As I left my hotel that morning, forcing my way with some violence through the crowd of Moslems offering their donkeys, I found myself walking in crooked, unpaved streets, on the ancient mould of the Nile, trodden by human feet since Cairo was first founded, and still almost as soft and elastic as a Turkey carpet. About me were flat-roofed houses, with projecting, covered balconies, a palm-tree here and there rising over them, or a minaret with its encircling balconies. It seemed as if I had been introduced at once into a dirty masquerade. I was among swarthy-bearded men, with glittering white teeth, passing to and fro on foot or on asses—men in turbans or close caps of every color, their feet in red or yellow slippers, or bare; their legs in loose blue or white bags, or concealed by a robe of striped silk, reaching to their feet, or by a long white shirt, over which was worn a black, brown, or green robe, with wide, flowing sleeves. Sometimes a Greek passed in his white petticoat, sometimes a priest of the Greek church, or an Armenian ecclesiastic in his ample black robe. Barefooted women in loose blue cotton gowns came in the crowd, bearing water-jars on their heads, or bundles of green clover freshly cut, and holding with one hand their coarse blue mantles closely over the lower part of the face. These were of the laboring class; but here and there was seen one of their more opulent sisters, moving along the street, in wide slippers, with a waddling gait— a pile of glistening silks or of white muslin, with a pair of eyes visible at the top, and on each side the tips of her fingers, where they held the mantle drawn closely over her forehead. Sometimes the lady was mounted astride on a donkey, with a domestic to hold her in her seat, and keep her from being jolted; her mantle, gathering the wind as she went, made her look like an enormous sack, placed upright on the saddle.

INTERIOR OF A HOUSE AT CAIRO.

Water-carriers, with their legs bare from the middle of the thigh downward, were driving asses laden with the water of the Nile in goat-skins. Sometimes a large procession of asses, carrying panniers filled with fresh masses of plaster of Paris, would block the way. At other times, in the narrower passages, we had to wait till half a score of camels had gone by, bearing on each side a block of stone just cut from the quarries, or an enormous beam of wood. Now and then the street was occupied with a train of carts—almost the only vehicle seen with wheels in Cairo. The wheels were singularly loose on the axles, and as they staggered along and wavered from side to side, threatened to knock down the unwary passenger. We passed through the bazars —as the streets occupied by the traders are called—over-canopied for the most part by mats stretched across from the uppermost stories, or by roofs of thin boards with openings for ventilation. Here sat the merchants of Cairo, cross-legged, in the dark little recesses which serve them as shops, some smoking, some chaffering volubly with their customers, some occupied in marking the articles they sold, a few lying asleep on their mats. In the open squares the barbers had brought out their mats and begun their work. Taking the head of a Mussulman between his knees and pulling off the turban, the squatting operator would ply his razor with surprising quickness of motion, and in a few minutes turn out the skull of his patient as smooth as a turnip. Here women were sitting in the dust, bare-legged, with bosoms more than half exposed under their loose garments, but with their faces concealed under a dirty rag, selling oranges and dates from broad, shallow baskets. Here squalid men, the filthiest of their race, were sitting with their backs against the walls, smoking, or sunning themselves, and in the angles of the buildings were young puppies huddling together where they were littered, while the prick-eared mother had left them to prowl for food or bark at the Frank stranger. Our arrival in one of these squares was sometimes the signal for a general chorus from all the dogs of the neighborhood.

As we went on, we peeped into the doors and windows of several of the mosques, of a venerable appearance without, but ill-built, ruinous, and ill-patched within, the carved wooden portions going to decay and dropping to the floor. In them squatted groups of the faithful on their mats, with rosaries in their hands, chanting their morning prayers. Near the mosques we often heard a clamorous chorus of shrill voices; it was from the schools, where the boys were committing their lessons to memory, by repeating them aloud.

From all the multitude engaged in these employments arose a perpetual noise, not of the clanking and humming of machinery, and the rattling of carriages, and the striking of iron hoofs on the pavement, as in our cities; but of human voices, greeting, arguing, jesting, laughing, shouting, scolding, cursing, praying, and begging, mingled with the bleating of camels, the braying of asses, and the barking of innumerable dogs. It is a mistake to speak of the Oriental as grave, solemn, and quiet; the Egyptian, at least, is the liveliest and noisiest of slaves. Everything in this country is done with noise. Two rowers never pull their oars, even for five minutes, without alternate chants and responses; not a stone is moved to its place in a building without the same accompaniment; the quarries east of Cairo resound with a shrill and ceaseless clamor of tongues. The most trivial affairs of life are the subject of discussions that seem to have no end. Every new object or new incident is a signal for a volley of words from old and young. The camel-driver sings all day to the animals he leads; and when he watches them by night in the desert, keeps himself awake by the exercise of his voice.

I was much struck with this chorus of sounds, when the other day I visited the citadel, and from the site of the magnificent mosque of Mohammed Ali, beheld the city below me with its swarming streets, and the fields and gardens of vivid green surrounding it, intersected with thronged roads. All around this scene of life and noise lay the silence and desolation of the desert—the vast Lybian desert to the west, with the everlasting pyramids at its edge, around which millions of human beings of the elder world sleep in their pits and caves;—and to the east, a desert as broad and still, on the skirts of which stand the tombs of the later sovereigns of Egypt among the graves of their subjects.

The mosque of which I have spoken is one of

THE FERRY AT OLD CAIRO.

the very finest works of Oriental architecture; but it is built under the superintendence of European architects, though with Egyptian materials, by the munificence of an Egyptian sovereign. A vast colonnade of Egyptian alabaster, in the Moorish style, surrounds the building and its court. You are struck at first with the lightness and airiness of its appearance, but you are somewhat disappointed when you perceive that the columns of this beautiful mosque are held in their place by a horizontal bar of iron, passing from capital to capital, and that each capital has also a transverse iron bar connecting it with the wall opposite. This expedient is a common one in Egyptian architecture, but the older mosques have bars of wood. No such disappointment awaits you when you enter the mosque itself. It is spacious and lofty, and the simplicity of its design gives to its amplitude and height their full effect. Four lofty half-domes rich with gildings, and resting on pilasters of polished alabaster, carry up the eye to a loftier and ampler dome in the midst, where rays of gold stream from a central point, and golden stars glitter on a blue ground. You have above you what reminds you of the glory and breadth of the firmament in a starlight night. The light from without comes through windows the glass of which is stained with the richest colors. In one of the corners is the tomb of Mohammed Ali, separated from the rest of the church by an enclosure, within which a group of Moslems were seen in prayer. The tomb itself was covered with a pile of Cashmere shawls. The mosque is not yet quite finished, and artisans are still at work within it.

It is almost the first business of travellers in Egypt to visit the pyramids of Ghizeh, and we made it ours; but do not suppose that I am going to weary you with a description of them. We set out on one of the glorious winter-days of Egypt, with a one-eyed dragoman at the head of our little train, brandishing a long stick, and attired in a costume which, though considerably the worse for wear, was very showy at a little distance. Three brown Arab boys in blue shirts, and close-fitting dirty white caps, came trotting and screaming after us to urge on the donkeys we rode. For two or three miles we kept along the Nile, among trees and gardens, and then crossed to the west bank in a boat manned by three men, one of whom, a fine-looking Arab, in a single garment of coarse white linen, handled the sail, and his two companions the oars. As they rowed, one sang, "God is great;" to which the other responded, "God-give me strength." Arriving on the other side, we rode through a village, where the dogs barked at us fiercely from the tops of the mud-cottages, and the dirty inhabitants, squatting by the way, clamored for *bakhshish*, as we appeared, the children running after us. We passed through a palm-grove where turtle-doves were flying about, and the hoopoe, a bird of beautifully-speckled plumage, descended in search of its food close to our path. Then we struck out upon the fields where the peasant women and children were watching their camels and buffaloes, tethered and grazing among the clover and crisp helva-grass. We came at length to where an ancient canal, now a broad hollow with a little water in it, wound along not far from the western edge of the fertile country. A score of Arabs, Bedouins from a neighboring village, came about us, prepared to carry us over on their shoulders. I could not but admire the fine figures of these men, with their muscular, shapely limbs, uniting strength with agility, and their striking countenances. A sculptor could not find a better model, as it seemed to me, for the perfection of the human form. Throwing off their upper garments, and fastening their lower ones considerably above the waist, two of these strapping fellows lifted me up by the legs, while I supported myself by the hands on their shoulders, and in this way waded with me through the mud and water. The others were carried over in the same manner, as well as a French gentleman and lady who had come up with us just as we were about to cross.

We were soon on the bare sands, ascending gradually to the range of rocks skirting the desert, on the brow of which the pyramids are placed. Of course we climbed to the top of the great pyramid. "If you no go up, what for you come to pyramid?" asked one of the Arabs, who spoke a little English, and the question seeming to me a very pertinent one. From the summit of this vast pile of hewn stones, which would cover all Washington Square with its base, we looked over the green Delta, stretching north, with dark groves spotting it like broad shadows of clouds. To the west of us was the Lybian desert, a waste of rocky hill-tops and sandy hollows; to the north rose the summits of pyramid after pyramid, and eastward lay Cairo, below the pinnacles of the mosque of Mohammed Ali, beyond which gleamed the white edge of another desert.

As I stood amidst the pyramids, where, all around, the skirts of the desert are one vast cemetery, full of tombs and mummy-pits, and remains of pyramids of smaller size, I could not but wonder that there should ever have arisen any doubt as to the design of these immense structures. They were meant as monuments of the dead, and, in my opinion, nothing more. They are the same in shape as some of the smaller monuments, and no more exceed them in size than the kings to whose memory they were erected, excelled in power and riches the most distinguished of their subjects.

A day or two afterward we visited the pyramids of Sakkara, lying to the north of those of Ghizeh. We had a letter to M. Mariette, who is here, employed by the French government in making excavations among the tombs and other remains of the ancient cemetery of Memphis. He received us very politely, and ordered the tomb of Apis to be lighted up for us. We descended into the rock by an inclined passage leading from a portal graven with numerous hieroglyphics. A gallery of about four hundred feet in length lay before us, regularly arched overhead, with chambers, at intervals on each side, the floor of which was about five feet below that of the gallery. Each of these chambers contained its sarcophagus of black or gray granite, exquisitely polished, about twelve feet in length, ten in height, and seven in width. They were covered with hieroglyphic characters. On each lay a massive lid of the same material, weighing tons, which, centuries since, had been shoved a little aside by iron levers, the marks of which are yet visible, giving us an opportunity of looking into the interior. It was empty. "This," said M. Mariette, " was done by the Persians, by order of their king, Cambyses, to show his contempt for the worship of the Egyptians."

One of the sarcophagi was found which had escaped the general desecration. M. Mariette had ordered it to be opened, and its contents

VIEW FROM PHILAE

were lying on the lid when I saw it. They were the bones of the sacred bull of the ancient Egyptians, the Apis, for which this tomb was destined. Every one of these enormous chests of stone had formerly contained similar remains, which, thousands of years since, had been dragged forth and scattered, and trampled upon, by a foreign soldiery from the north.

We slept that night in a chamber of M. Mariette's house, a building which he said had cost him eleven francs. Its walls were made of the unburnt brick, part of the structures of earlier ages, which his workmen had dug from the sands, and it was roofed over with logs of the palm-tree. In the morning we looked at the excavations made by M. Mariette in front of the tomb of Apis, revealing the remains of an extensive temple of white marble, which he has identified as the Egyptian temple of Serapis. Here are pedestals of columns, the lower part of walls, and other remains of a sumptuous edifice long covered up in sand. Strabo speaks of the sand as drifting into the courts of this temple in his time. "It must have been the same from the first," said M. Mariette ; " the temple itself rests on a base of sand."

The excavations had been suspended for a day or two when I visited Sakkara, but they were soon to be resumed. Three or four hundred workmen are generally employed; and objects of ancient workmanship are frequently found, of an interesting character, which are immediately packed up and sent to the museums of Paris. "These men," said M. Mariette, "whom I have with me, are the fellahs, the peasantry of the neighborhood, not the Bedouins, for it is not easy to make the Bedouin engage in any regular employment. These fellahs work hard, receive small wages, live on little, and are faithful, good-tempered, and cheerful. They are the same patient race which built the pyramids."

Not far from the tomb of Apis is a village inhabited by Bedouins. "I am obliged," said M. Mariette, "to keep watch against the men of that tribe. These fellahs, whom you heard singing all last night to keep themselves awake, are my watchmen. About eighteen months since the Bedouins attacked the place in the night, armed with their matchlocks, a clumsy weapon, with which they did not succeed in doing any harm. We disarmed them, took them prisoners, and brought them before the authorities; but they were released on the ground that I had no right to be here, and that they committed no crime in attempting to drive me off. Since that time an understanding has been had with the Egyptian government, and this enterprise is now under its protection."

"These Bedouins," pursued M. Mariette, "as well as those fine-looking fellows whom you saw at Ghizeh, were settled in these villages by Mehemet Ali. It was his policy to allure them to settle in regular communities, and to quit their roving life. He assigned them these lands which they now cultivate, and exempted them from many of the burdens borne by the fellahs, but which a Bedouin would not endure. Formerly these men would commit robberies and assassinations, and then hide themselves in the desert, where it was vain to pursue them. Now, if any of them are guilty of crimes, the government has them in its power. They intermarry with the fellahs, and their character is undergoing a gradual change."

We visited at Sakkara one of the repositories of the mummies of the sacred bird Ibis. It was a long passage cut in the rock of the desert, with branches in various directions, full of earthen jars, about a foot and a half in length, in which these mummies are contained. Every traveller, as a matter of course, brings out and breaks one of these jars, and we followed the general practice. In some of them we found only a handful of brown dust and two or three lumps of bitumen, wrapped in folds of linen cloth, which looked as if scorched by fire, and fell to pieces on being touched; in others the wrappings were tolerably white, and on being unrolled showed the figure of the bird tolerably perfect, with all its bones, its beak, and even its feathers in tolerable preservation. The ground around the spot was strewn, to a considerable distance, with fragments of these jars and pieces of mummy-cloths, and among them were here and there portions of human mummies, a skull, a thigh-bone, blackened with bitumen, or a torn part of the cloth in which the corpse had been swathed. Hollows nearly filled with sand, showed where recent excavations in search of tombs and mummy-pits had been made; but the government, I hear, has prohibited all such undertakings for the future.

After examining a tomb in the precipice overhanging the plain of the Nile, the chambers of which, cut in the living rock, are graven with colored hieroglyphics, we returned to Cairo by way of Memphis. Descending the height, we followed a high causey, built of the fine dark mould of the region, through fields green with crops, to the village of Mitrahenny. It stands in the midst of an extensive circle of mounds, from three to thirty feet in height, which are all that remain of the renowned metropolis of Egypt in the time of its early splendor. These mounds appear at first to be of the dark earth which forms the soil of the plain, but on looking more nearly you perceive that they are heaps of unburnt brick, among which a few burnt bricks are scattered. A vast grove of palms, with trenches leading to their roots for the purpose of irrigation, overshadows them, and extends to a considerable distance on every side. In the midst is a shallow pool of water, over which I saw the kingfisher hovering and striking his prey, and beside it the women of the village were filling their water-jars. The branches of the palms were rustling pleasantly in the morning breeze, and birds of various kinds were flitting about with little fear of man, for the people of this country are not allowed to carry arms. Among them was the beautiful hoopoe, seeking its food at the roots of trees, sometimes erecting its brilliant crest into a semicircle, and then laying it backward in a long slender pencil, so as to seem almost another bird.

Beside the little lake, the ancient reservoir doubtless of the city of Memphis, stood a tent, the tent of Hakakyin Bey—I hope I have the right orthography of his name—an Armenian, formerly interpreter to Mohammed Ali, who possesses a taste for antiquarian researches. He has made several excavations in this spot, uncovering a colossal statue of granite lying on its face, and several smaller figures, one or two of them the most pleasing samples of ancient Egyptian statuary to be seen here, and that is not saying much in their praise. They stand ranged on each side of the entrance to the tent, into which we were permitted to enter and take our lunch, the proprietor being absent.

Such is Memphis now, the once great city to which Martial attributes the building of the pyramids, those miracles of barbaric art, *barbara mi-*

racula, as he calls them. Seen from its site, they appear to stand around it in a semicircle, from those of Dashour on the south to those of Ghizeh on the north. Its builders wrought for the present age in a way they little dreamed of. I could not imagine at first to what cause it was owing that these mounds, apparently of the same rich mould which composed the soil of the plain, were wholly barren of herbage, even in those parts which were irrigated by the trenches conveying water to the palms. On examining their surface, I found it covered in many parts with a nitrous effervescence, looking at a little distance like hoar-frost. The soil is everywhere highly impregnated with nitre—so highly as to prevent the growth of plants, except where it is washed by the annual overflow of the Nile. How they contrive to make the palm grow in places where no other vegetable will take root, I am sure I cannot tell. In emerging from the forest of these trees, in the midst of which lie the mounds of Memphis, we come to a small circle of mounds almost as high, through which our road lay. It was a manufactory of saltpetre, conducted by the government. The earth which forms the mounds of Memphis is brought hither in panniers slung on the backs of asses, and steeped in the waters of the Nile; the water in which it is infused is evaporated in broad, shallow vats, and the residue is crude saltpetre. In one sense, therefore, the ancient inhabitants of Memphis may be said to have built for posterity.

LETTER VII.

Passage in a steamer up the Nile to Thebes and the lower cataract of the Nile.—Arrangements for the voyage.—Beauty of the weather.—Upper Egypt, its aspect.—Irrigation.—Villages.—Scarcity of fruit-trees.—Rocky hills overlooking the narrow valley of the Nile.—The Temples of Thebes and Karnac.—A French excavator, M. Mounier.—Uncovering of old temples.—Tyranny of the Egyptian authorities.—A Latin convent.—Copts.—Their church.

CAIRO, EGYPT, January 30th, 1853.

WHEN we were just ready to set out for Sakkara, we learned that a party was making up to visit Thebes and Philæ in a government steamer, which was to go and return in seventeen days. The price for each passenger was two thousand eight hundred piastres, or about one hundred and fifty dollars of our money; and as soon as twelve passengers could be found, the steamer immediately was to proceed up the Nile. We had already concluded a bargain with a dragoman, as the men who engage in these undertakings are called, to convey us over the smaller Arabian desert to Jerusalem, and thence to one of the seaports of Syria. He was to provide us with the means of seeing all the most interesting places and objects on the journey, which was to begin on the 13th of January. But the temptation of seeing Upper Egypt, with its magnificent monuments of a remote antiquity, in less than three weeks, was too strong to be resisted. We therefore added our names to those of the passengers already engaged. The requisite number was soon completed. We found means to induce our dragoman to wait for our return, and on the very day when we should have started with him for Jerusalem, we left Cairo in the steamer for Essuan, just below the first cataract of the Nile, and within a short distance of the island of Philæ.

Hitherto the voyage up the Nile has generally been performed in boats driven by sails. These are well fitted up for the purpose with comfortable cabins, but with calms or contrary winds the voyage becomes extremely tedious, and its duration is always uncertain. We passed these boats frequently on the river, overtaking or meeting them, and sometimes found them moored to the shore where we stopped. There were four or five on the Nile bearing the American flag, and as in our party of fifteen there were nine Americans to four Englishmen and one Frenchman, we ran up, by common consent, the American flag also. Our party was probably the first which had made the voyage to Upper Egypt with a satisfactory degree of comfort. The steamer had just been fitted up expressly for these voyages, with a separate chamber for each passenger, which had never been the case in any of the Nile steamers before; the furniture was new and perfectly clean; our larder was abundantly stored, though the cookery was not the most skilful; and the waiters, Greeks and Smyrniotes, were attentive and obliging. We had an ill-looking Bulgarian for a captain, who seemed, however, to understand his duty pretty well; a Scotch Highlander for an engineer, and a crew of good-natured Arabs, of whom it generally took four to manage the helm.

We left Cairo on a beautiful evening, performed our voyage to the lower cataract of the Nile in sixteen instead of seventeen days—for the steamer outstripped the estimates which had been made of her passage from place to place, and here we are again at Cairo. We could not have wished for finer weather, with the exception of one sultry day, in which, however, the steamer kept on her passage. The temperature was that of an English summer; the sky always clear, the evenings like those of Italy at the finest season, a blaze of orange-colored light brightening every object and illuminating every recess; the nights refreshing and without mosquitoes, which torment us so much at Cairo; and the mornings cool—sometimes, I confess, quite unpleasantly so for those who had, as was my case, their cabins on deck. We took our meals on deck, under an awning, and before breakfast was ready the temperature had become quite genial, so quickly did the rays of the sun warm that transparent atmosphere. The temper of our party was as pleasant and genial as the weather; I doubt whether mere chance ever threw together a better-natured and more obliging set of men.

Upper Egypt is easily described. It is a narrow belt of verdure, stretching from the Delta far south into the desert. A river of turbid water rushes swiftly through its whole length, on the sand-banks of which stalk flocks of cormorants and pelicans, with here and there a crocodile basking in the sun—a timid monster which slides into the water at the first notice he has of the approach of man. On each shore, within a

LUXOR FROM THE WATER.

short distance of each other, wheels moved by buffaloes and donkeys, or buckets suspended to a pole which turns on a pivot, and lifted by peasants naked to the waist, shaded from the sun by a screen of palm-leaves, distribute over the fields, at all seasons except that of the annual flood, the waters to which the country owes its three crops a year. From time to time, a town or village, built of unburnt bricks, formed from the mould of the fields, mixed with chopped straw, rises on the banks of the river, resounding with the shrill cries of children. The poorer and lazier portion of the population are seen basking and smoking by the walls of the dwellings, and overhead are aviaries full of flocks of pigeons, for the convenience of which, an additional story is built on many of the housetops. The villages are always near, and sometimes within, a lofty grove of date-palms, which supplies the inhabitants with food, and the tending of which, in conducting the water to their roots, forms part of their occupation. Of other trees there are few; here and there, perhaps, a broad sycamore, or a thick-leaved cassia, or a tamarind; but in Upper Egypt trees seem never to be planted for shade; even fruit-trees, with the exception of the palm, are rare, and a little distance south of Cairo, the country most congenial to their growth, the orange-gardens disappear, and the banana is never seen.

On each side a range of rocky hills without a shrub or plant, sometimes approaching close to the river, and sometimes retreating to form a plain of considerable extent on its border, overlooks this fertile tract. At their base is generally a hard, gravelly level, or a sheet of loose sand, a little elevated above the meadows, and always bare of herbage, but at times they flank the river, with a long wall of sandstone or granite. Old sepulchres yawn in their sides, and kites and eagles sail above them. One morning on my excursion to Upper Egypt, I crossed the gravelly waste near Beni Hassan, and climbed what seemed to be the highest peak in the range to the east of the river. All before me, as far as the sight could extend to the eastward, the region was broken into rough pinnacles of rock, with narrow valleys and passes filled with loose sand.

I will not tire you with describing what has

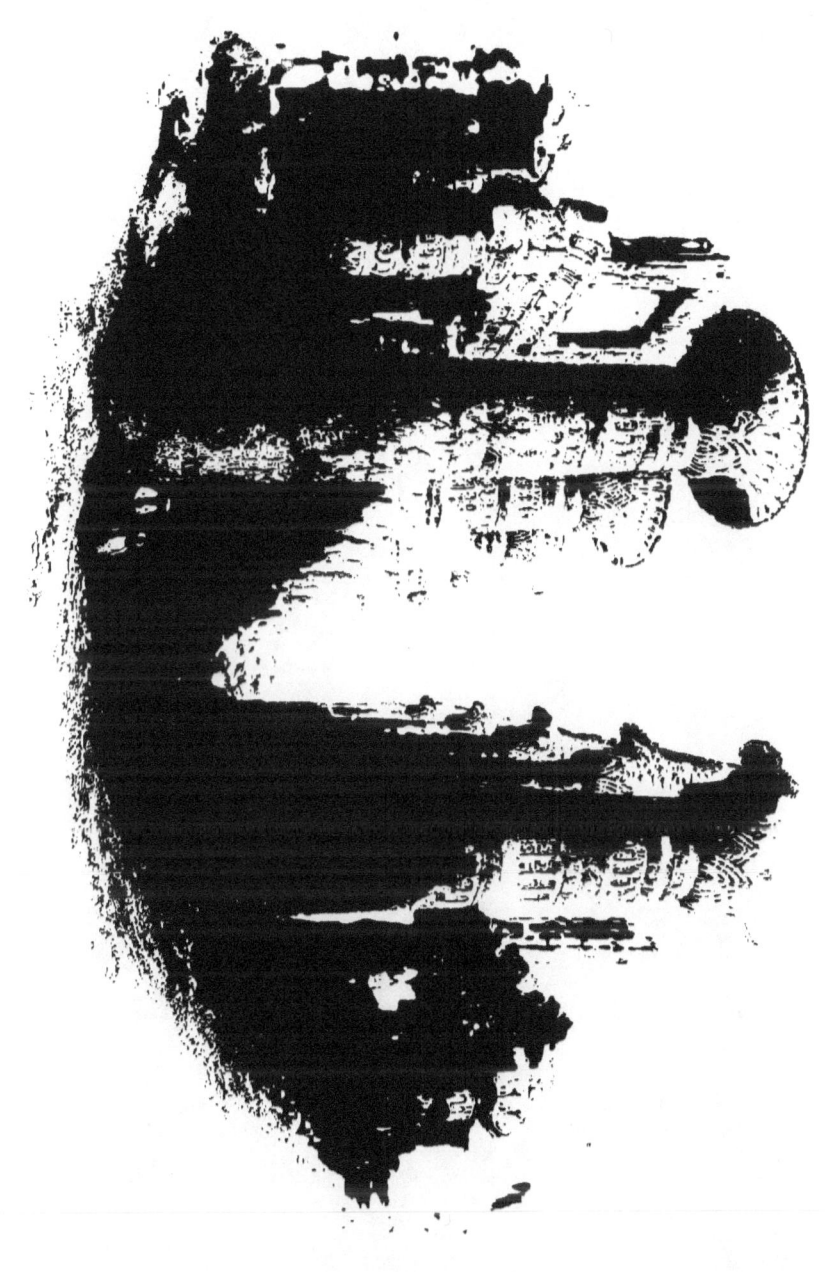

been so often described—the ancient tombs and temples of Upper Egypt. The grandest of them all are the remains of Thebes, consisting of the temples at Karnac and Luxor, and the tombs and colossal statues on the other side of the river. As I sat among the forest of gigantic columns in the great court of the temple at Karnac, it appeared to me that after such a sight no building reared by human hands could affect me with a sense of sublimity. Seen through the vista of columns to the east was a small grove of palms close to the ruins, and another to the west; their tall and massive trunks looked slender and low, compared to the enormous shafts of stone around me. I looked up to where the clouds, floating slowly over, seemed almost to touch them with their skirts, and perceived that two or three of them, shaken perhaps by an earthquake from their upright position, stood leaning against their fellows, still bearing upon their capitals portions of the enormous architrave which belonged to them. Thus they have stood, and thus they doubtless will stand for ages; scarce anything, but another earthquake, can bring them to the ground. The spoilers of this vast temple, extending over miles of surface, the annihilators of its rows of sphinxes, and the destroyers of its magnificent colonnades, seem to have confined their work of mischief to those parts of it less massively built, and to have shrunk from attempting to overthrow the columns of the great court.

At Thebes we found M. Mounier, a French artist, who is employed by the Pacha to clear away the rubbish from the temples of Upper Egypt. I was walking along the shore, near to his boat, with two gentlemen of our party, when he perceived us from the cabin, and coming out upon the deck, politely invited us to enter. Of course we did not refuse. Many of the finest of the ancient temples of Egypt, that for example at Esneh, are half buried in heaps of earth, accumulated from age to age by the mud cottages built within them by successive generations of the peasantry. The larger portion of the magnificent temple at Esneh is actually filled by them to the roof, and the fellahs are now building on the roof itself.

"My business," said M. Mounier, "is to cause these people to leave the temples, and then to clear them entirely of rubbish, both within and

PLAIN OF THEBES

without. The temple at Edfoo and that at Denderah were partly cleared, by order of Mohammed Ali, a few years since, but all that was removed from the interior was heaped about the walls, so that no idea could be formed of the effect of their exterior."

M. Mounier had already uncovered and excavated a very fine portion of the temple of Luxor, to which he conducted us. He informed us that he generally had about three hundred workmen employed. "I have," he continued, "the authority of the government to make requisitions on each of the villages in turn for a certain number of laborers, who are bound to work a certain number of days. Such objects of curiosity, works of art, domestic utensils, etc., as I find in these excavations, I send immediately to Cairo, where the Pasha is forming a museum. As fast as the different temples are completely uncovered, I make drawings of them, which are hereafter to be engraved and published in a volume."

In the cabin of M. Mounier's boat we found Madame Mounier, an elegant French lady, who assists her husband by taking photographic views of the temples, and copying them on drawing paper, a pursuit by which she said she beguiled the years of exile from her native country.

I inquired of M. Mounier if the workmen employed by him on the ruins were paid. He replied that they were not. "I have made up my mind, however," he added, "to advise the Pasha to give them wages. The expense would not be great, as the wages of a laborer are but thirty paras a day, and they would work much more cheerfully and diligently if they were paid."

Thirty paras, you must understand, are about four cents of our money. I shall be glad to learn hereafter that M. Mounier has succeeded in persuading the Egyptian government to treat its subjects a little less like slaves. Its manner of proceeding is extremely summary. As I have mentioned, the steamer in which we went up the Nile belonged to the government. A little before arriving at Siout, our captain had occasion for a pilot. He pounced upon a boat and took out three persons, whom he compelled to serve in that capacity till he arrived at Siout, where he procured from the local authorities an order compelling the most expert of them to act as pilot so long as he was wanted. At Ghizeh, some miles further south, we stopped to take in coal. Two men in red slippers, with long staves, came driving on, like cattle, the barefooted peasants who were to weigh the coal lying in woollen sacks on the shore, and carry it on their shoulders to our steamer. Our captain himself performed the functions of his office under fear of the bastinado. It happened that Abbas Pasha, the Viceroy of Egypt, was himself on a voyage up the Nile in a steamer, for the purpose of collecting tribute at the time of an excursion to Essuan. On his way up the river, he found a government steamer aground, an accident which often happens on the Nile, and which had happened two or three times to our own steamer. The Pasha ordered the captain to be taken out of his boat and soundly bastinadoed.

One of the most interesting incidents of our voyage was a visit we paid to the Coptic community of Negadeh, on the west bank of the Nile, about four hundred miles above Cairo. We landed at their little town before breakfast, and proceeded to the Latin convent, the superior of which, in a red turban and Arab dress, received us with great civility. He was a Neapolitan, who had resided in the country seventeen years. He showed us the church of his convent, one of those crazy edifices, with rude Moorish columns, which are so common in Egypt, and the several parts of which seem with difficulty to hang together. He then passed us over to several respectable looking men in white turbans and black gowns, who, we understood, were Coptic priests. When they were told that we were Christians, from the distant land of America, who had called to pay them our respects, they expressed their satisfaction at this mark of regard, and seemed desirous to pay us every possible attention. They took us to their place of worship, through an open court, used as a school, in which the boys, squatting on the dusty pavement, were learning to read and write from a lesson written with ink in Coptic and Arabic, on a leaden tablet. The Copts are the clerks and scribes of Egypt. The church was of the same class of edifices with the Latin one. As we entered, the morning service was near its close, and the priest, in reciting its last words, took the hands of several of the worshippers between his own. Both in this and the Latin church were screens of lattice-work, behind which the female worshippers concealed themselves; for the custom of seclusion among the women is national, and is almost as strong among the Copts as among the Mussulmans. From behind these lattices we could observe female figures silently departing. The priests showed us their books in the Coptic language, and attended us to our steamer. I believe the boys had been let out of the schools on our account, for of a sudden the beach was thronged with a great, but most quiet and well-behaved multitude, as if the whole male population of the place, young and old, had been suddenly assembled to do us honor. At our express desire, three of the priests were allowed to come on board and look at the steamer, after which they took their leave; we moved from the shóre, and left the crowd gazing upon us in silence. During the whole of our visit, not a single person of our party was asked for money: it was the only instance of this sort of reserve which we met with in all Egypt.

We are now on the point of crossing what they call here the Little Arabian Desert, on our way to Palestine.

LETTER VIII.

Journey from Cairo to Jerusalem across the Little Desert.—Gardens enclosed by the prickly pear.—Olive-trees.—Sycamore of the Virgin.—The Obelisk of Heliopolis.—Village of Khankia.—Lake of the Pilgrims.—Brief twilight.—Journey on camels.—Hoopoes.—Entrance on the Desert.—Our dragoman.—The father of couriers.—Furniture of our caravan.—Ground strewn with fragments of pottery.—An Arab burial-ground.—Village of Belbays.

JERUSALEM, PALESTINE, Feb. 22d, 1853.

OUR arrangements being completed for the journey from Cairo to Jerusalem, by way of what is here called the Little Desert or the Shorter Desert, our dragoman sent forward his camels with the baggage in the morning, and in the afternoon we set out on donkeys. On leaving the town, we passed among gardens fenced by rows of the prickly pear, which here grows to an enormous size. You know its peculiar mode of growth—one broad oval leaf, bristling with spines, proceeding from another; but as the plant becomes old the lower leaves take a rounded form, run into each other, and form large crooked trunks of a dark-brown color. They make a hedge which neither man nor beast can penetrate. Beyond the gardens we entered a country of green fields, where the road was planted on each side with the sycamore, or Egyptian fig, the acacia, and the tamarisk, all in full foliage. Sometimes our way led us among the lofty stems of a palm-grove, with its numerous trenches, dry at that season, for conducting water to the roots of the trees. The road was full of people—men leading loaded camels, women with water-jars on their heads, or fagots of dry branches, and people of both sexes on donkeys. One of these, kicking his donkey's sides to make him keep pace with us, would occasionally join our party and hold a conversation with our dragoman and his companions.

It was only on this road that I saw the olive-tree growing in Egypt. On a large estate belonging to some distinguished Egyptian, who wears the title of Pasha, and whose name I beg his pardon for having forgotten, the culture of the olive has been introduced or perhaps revived. I have never seen finer orchards of the tree than those which, at the distance of twelve or fifteen miles from Cairo, shaded the soil to a great extent, on both sides of the way; they were young, but not too young for an abundant fruitage, and were growing luxuriantly. It was evident that they were well watered, for in two or three places, where irrigation had apparently been neglected, I saw some plantations of the olive which had not a very thriving appearance.

Our conductor turned aside from the main road, and led us to a garden on the same estate, full of orange, citron, and pomegranate trees, with a few roses and other flowering plants. "In this garden," said he, "is the sycamore tree under which the Virgin rested with her child, in her flight to Egypt. It is much visited by pilgrims, and a jar of sweet water is kept standing by it for their sake." We were admitted to the garden by the Arabs who tended it, and saw the tree, a fine sample of the old sycamores of the country, with an enormous leaning stem, and a scanty circumference of boughs, looking as if it had survived several centuries. By its side was a large earthen jar, with water for the pilgrims. It is one of the principal works of Mussulman piety and charity to supply the traveller with water. Jars of water are kept in little niches at the tombs of the Santons, and charitable people when they die, instead of endowing an hospital, leave a legacy to set up a fountain.

In another garden we stopped to see the obelisk of Heliopolis, a beautiful shaft of polished red granite, standing upright where it has stood for thousands of years, while the temples by which it was surrounded have long ago disappeared. Only a few fragments of their cornices and columns remain to attest that they once existed.

Toward sunset we overtook our camels, and pitched our tent just beyond the village of Khankia, among some scattered palms. The spot was full of wells, and the work of drawing water for the thirsty fields was carried on with great activity; the *sakkia* or wheel, turned by buffaloes, was creaking, and the *shadoof*, or pole and bucket, was going up and down. Near us was an old mosque, apparently just ready to fall into ruins, as is the case with all the mosques in Egypt. A few curious villagers gathered around us to see our people set up their tents, and our cook make his preparations for dinner. We strolled to a little lake near the village, named *Birket el Hoj*, or Lake of the Pilgrims. It is on the way from Cairo to Mecca, and is probably so called because the pilgrims here lay in their provision of water before crossing the desert. We found it a shallow sheet of water, with a gravelly shore, where camels were drinking, and women washing their feet and filling their water-jars. The day had been beautiful—a genial summer temperature, the sunshine tempered by clouds—and the sun now went down in a glow of orange-colored light. A short twilight succeeded—the twilight is always short in Egypt—the women hastened away from the lake, the *sakkia* ceased to creak, the *shadoof* was still, and darkness was upon us before we returned to our tent.

Next morning we sent back our donkeys to Cairo, and prepared for a journey on the backs of camels. The villagers were again on the ground to see us strike our tents, and several hoopoes came down from the palms, and ran about gleaning the scattered grains left where the camels had been fed. This beautiful bird, unfortunately for itself, is a game-bird, and our dragoman shot two of them. The camels were kneeling on the ground, the more impatient of them having their fore-legs tied under them, to prevent their rising, and were uttering a harsh, angry bleat, as the loads were put on their backs.

At length we were ready; I placed myself on the back of the camel destined for me, and was nearly thrown over his back, and then over his head, as he lifted me by three different jerks to the height of nine feet in the air. We left the village, passing by the Lake of the Pilgrims, and entered the desert, which here was a vast plain of hard ground, strewn with pebbles.

Our caravan consisted of thirteen camels, tethered to each other, and walking in a row. By the side of one of them trotted a young donkey, and on the back of another, among some baggage, sat a monkey from Nubia, not yet quite tamed, and making a fearful grimace every time he was approached. Four Arabs from El Areesh, a little town in the desert, on the seashore, walked with the camels; they were the owners of the animals, and one of them guided the first of the troop by a halter.

At our head, armed with a long sabre and carrying a rifle, rode Emanuel Balthas, our dragoman, an Athenian by birth, speaking the ancient Greek as well as the Romaic, fluent in Italian, Turkish and Arabic, intelligible in French, and in a fair way to learn English, which he was picking up very fast from those with whom he travelled. If any of my countrymen should have occasion for a dragoman in Syria or Egypt, I can with a safe conscience refer them to Emanuel Balthas, a little man, with the manners of a nobleman, active, prompt, anxious to satisfy his employers, as choleric and as generous as a prince, a little too much given to flogging his Arabs, but always attaching them to him by the liberality with which he treats them. He engaged, for a Napoleon a day from each of us, to provide us with conveyance, shelter, beds, and food, in our journey across the desert and through Syria, paying our expenses at Jerusalem, Damascus, and the other places we might have occasion to visit, till we should reach Jaffa or some other seaport on the Mediterranean.

The rest of our party consisted of four American travellers, myself included; John Muscat, our courier, the father of couriers, as he called himself, and the most honest of his tribe, a native of the little island of Malta, fertile in men, which has its representatives in every port of the Mediterranean, from Gibraltar to Scanderoon; Gianneco, the cousin of our dragoman, a Smyr-

niote Greek, with a brow like that of the bust of
Hippocrates; and lastly, Vincenzo, our cook, a
Roman, whose whole soul was in his art, who
plucked his chickens as he sat on his camel, and
had no worldly ambition higher than that of
hearing his dinners praised. I doubt whether
such capital dinners as he gave us are often eaten
in the desert. Our camels carried two tents, one
for the travellers, the other for our dragoman
and his companions; four camp bedsteads, with
mattresses, pillows, and bedclothes; a table; four
camp-stools; mats and carpets for the floor of
our tent; a water-cask; a provision-chest, with
table-linen, tin plates, and knives and forks;
three small furnaces, with a supply of charcoal
and kitchen utensils; a hen-coop, crowded with
chickens, and a small crate filled with oranges.
Our Arabs had their blankets on their camels,
and passed the night with them in the open air.
I have mentioned the rifle and sabre carried by
our dragoman, but these were not his only weap-
ons; there was, besides, a pair of horse-pistols,
ready loaded, and the father of the couriers, on
the morning of our departure, had astonished us
by making his appearance equipped with a sword

of Persian manufacture, short and thick, like himself, which he now wore, and was ready to employ, as he assured us, against the brigands with which the road to Syria was beset. With such ample arrangements for our comfort and security, we entered with stout hearts upon our journey over the desert.

We dismounted from our camels at half-past twelve, to take our lunch. Mats were spread for us on the ground, and we shaded ourselves from the sun by umbrellas, while we took a short repast, sitting as well as we could in the oriental manner, or reclining on the ground. My camel was a vicious animal, bleating horribly whenever he was made to kneel or to rise, and occasionally offering to bite. I declined remounting him again for the day, but went on foot till we halted for the night. It was an easy matter to keep pace with the camels; they walk at the rate of about three miles an hour, and eight hours, or twenty-four miles, is the ordinary day's journey of a caravan like ours. Our way was on the skirt of the desert, with the palm-trees of the cultivated land in sight on one hand, and the hills of the desert on the other. All day, on looking back, the rocky heights immediately east of Cairo were in full view, with the mosque of Mohammed Ali and its tall minarets gleaming on their western edge.

At every step we set our feet among small fragments of pottery thickly strewn among the gravel—the only vestiges of the millions of human beings by whom this barren waste had been trodden since Egypt was first peopled.

In the course of the day we saw the glimmer of water to the northwest of us. It was a part of the ancient canal of Arsinöe, which reached from the Nile to the Red Sea. Toward sunset, a village of dark-colored mud houses, with white minarets of stone rising over them, appeared in sight, surrounded by palms, and I found myself in the midst of an Arab burial-ground; for the old practice of burying the dead in the desert is still common throughout Egypt. They were vaults of brick, underground, some of them fallen in; those which were entire were each surrounded by a narrow piece of masonry, about six feet in height, composed of bricks or stones laid in a crumbling kind of cement, and none of them bore inscriptions. Another hour's walk through loose sand brought me to a circle of mounds of dark mould, wholly bare of herbage, among which stands the little village of Belbays, on the site of an ancient town. Within this circle, under some palm-trees, we set up our tents. A caravan of Egyptians was already on the ground; they had unloaded their camels, spread their mats, and disposing their bales of goods around them, were preparing to pass the night in the open air. I find it recorded in my notes that this evening, in this wretched place, Vincenzo gave us the very best dinner we had eaten in Egypt.

LETTER IX.

Second, third, fourth, fifth, and sixth days of our journey.—A visit from two Arab women.—Coquetry of the younger.—Horsemanship of the Arabs.—A belt of cultivation in the Desert.—Rassel Wady.—Flocks of birds.—Irrigation.—Arabs singing.—A dragoman flogs an Arab.—A camel runs away.—A mirage.—Barook.—Pilgrims from Mecca.—A sirocco.—Dead camels.—A monkey digging sorrel.—Violence of the wind.—Our tents overturned at night.—Gatieh.—Personal appearance of the Arabs.—Vermin.

JERUSALEM, PALESTINE, Feb. 22d, 1853.

OUR tents were struck at sunrise, and we breakfasted in the open air, the wonder of several spectators from the village, who came to see the monkey and the Franks. As they approached a little too near the provision chest and other goods of the caravan, our dragoman drove them off with a fierce shout, and a flourish of his long cowskin. An old woman and a young one came to gather the camels' dung, which is used here for fuel, and the remains of barley and chopped straw with which the camels had been fed. The old woman asked alms; her young companion amused us by an exhibition of innocent coquetry. On her tawny but plump right arm she wore a bracelet of some cheap metal, and on her right hand three rings of the same material. In the intervals of her occupation, she covered the lower part of her face, which was not an unpleasing one, with her blue cotton mantle; but was careful to keep that brown handsome arm with its ornaments in full sight, resting it on her basket.

In the mean time, a muster of cavalry was going on at the gate of a large enclosure opposite our camping-ground. Now and then a horseman would strike his spurs into the side of the animal he rode, dash forward swiftly for a few rods, stop suddenly, wheel and dash forward again as swiftly, brandishing his carbine, while the horse's mane and tail streamed in the air. "Those soldiers," said the dragoman, "are going to El Areesh; their business is to keep the road of the desert clear of robbers. Three hundred of them are to be sent forward in the course of the day." Several small parties of these horsemen left the village before us, and when we at length mounted our camels and entered the desert, we found the road full of them. They soon, however, left us behind.

I had a better camel to-day; an exemplary animal in all respects save one—he was not satisfied to remain long in a kneeling position, and was apt to rise before he was bid. The motion of the camel, tossing its rider backward and forward, is at first extremely fatiguing; and it is customary to wear a belt, by which the muscles of the back are supported, while making these journeys. Our party had all provided themselves with these belts; but as I found that I could avoid the fatigue by varying my position on the back of the animal, sitting sometimes astride, sometimes with both legs on one side and sometimes on the other, and occasionally dismounting to walk, I laid my belt aside after the second day.

It was with no little delight that, toward the end of a day's journey over the herbless plain, we found ourselves again entering among green fields. A narrow tract of cultivation stretched far into the desert, a long cape of verdure putting out from the Delta, and we were crossing it at a place called Rassel Wady. Here were trenches of transparent brackish water, rippled by the wind; marshy spots producing a luxuriant crop of weeds; cotton-fields with bolls ready to be gathered, and a few trees. The reeds and trees were bending with the weight of hundreds of small birds perched upon them, keeping up a chorus of twitterings; and larger game-birds were hovering about in great numbers. There are two reasons why birds abound in Egypt: in the first place, the people are not allowed to own arms; and secondly, the Mussulman is tender of the lives of animals, never taking them wantonly. Balthas could not resist the temptation of adding to the stores of his larder, and getting down from his camel, began a war upon the birds. He shot several hoopoes and plovers, a pigeon, and a beautiful black and white bird—jetty black, and glistening white—which he called the *kinkinazo*.

Beside our way stood a tower of stone, one of a line of telegraphic stations established by Mohammed Ali, between Syria and Egypt, but now disused. Near it were the ruins of a village, roofless walls of unburnt brick, among which our road wound for awhile, and then emerging, passed by orange-gardens richly loaded with fruit. We were soon in the desert again, or rather passing between barren ground on one side, and luxuriant barley-fields on the other. These fields were kept fresh by little rills of water raised by a wheel from a neighboring well, one of which had overflowed its channel, and softened the earth for a little way in our path. One of our loaded camels was incautiously allowed to step into the moistened place; as soon as he touched it with his feet, he slipped and fell heavily to the ground. The Arabs took off his load, and after some floundering he was made to rise.

We pitched our tents on the clean gravel, and filled our cask with sweet but turbid water from a canal which was said to come from the Nile. Our Arabs sang, as they called it, all night, making a monotonous quavering sound, both guttural and nasal. They sang, I was told the next morning, to keep themselves awake while they watched the camels and the tents. Small parties of cavalry occasionally passed us in the night, on their way to El Areesh. "They keep the road clear of robbers," said our courier, "and are themselves the greatest robbers of all."

Next morning our road proceeded for several miles along the northern border of the green tract I have mentioned, which is a little lower than the adjacent desert on both sides. One of our camels dropped a part of his load, which had beed badly adjusted by the Arabs. Two of them immediately ran to replace it; and Balthas, jumping to the ground, flew at them with his cowskin, with which he dealt them several vigorous blows. Meantime the camel shook the rest of his load to the ground, and breaking into a gallop, scoured away over the desert, and was soon out of sight. The Arab who accompanied him, a well-limbed man, and a good runner, took after him, and was soon out of sight also. The chests and bags which had fallen were distributed among the other camels, and we went on, turning away from the green fields, of which we now took our last look. The day was somewhat sultry; a chain of arid hills rose to the southeast, and before us, from time to time, appeared the illusion so common in the desert, of lakes or pools of water, with trees on their borders reflected in the seeming fluid, where there was only a waste of gravel and stunted shrubs. After travelling for some miles, we overtook our runaway camel, with his Arab, and compelled him, notwithstanding his loud cries of remonstrance, to take his proper load. We encamped that night in the desert, at some distance from any human habitation, but a fire which we saw in the evening, at the distance of a mile or two, showed that there was another encampment in our neighborhood.

An hour's journey the following day brought us to a little hollow, in which were some remains of dwellings, a well, a few stumps of palms, and several young trees of the same kind. After we had filled our water-vessels, I walked on, over a tract of fine sand, among numerous little hillocks tufted with shrubs. I amused myself with observing the tracks of large and small birds, of lizards and jackals, on the smooth surface. We lunched in a place where we were attacked by a swarm of sand-flies, indicating that the sands had been steeped by a recent rain. The shrubs grew more numerous as we went on, and finally we halted for the night at a place called Barook by the Arabs, who have a name for every place in the desert, where there is water, or a palm-tree, or an eminence, or a hollow. At Barook there is a well of brackish water, and we saw the signs of many previous encampments—heaps of ashes from fires made with shrubs growing around, and innumerable foot-prints of camels and horses. In my walk this day, I observed several small plants in flower, feebly rooted in the sand, and I gathered a peculiar species of sorrel, with thick, juicy, brittle leaves.

The next day, as we were about to set out on our journey, two men, a mulatto and a young Arab, made their appearance and lighted a fire near us. They were pilgrims, they said, returning from Mecca, and had yet two days to walk before reaching their homes. They had eaten nothing, they told us, for the last twenty-four hours. Our provisions were all packed up and on the backs of camels, but we found half a chicken for them and an orange, which they seemed to accept gladly. One of our Arabs became offended at the manner in which his camel was loaded, took off its burden and rode forward upon the animal by himself. We set out in the midst of a strong wind, which had begun to blow before sunrise, and shifted toward the south as the day wore on, till it became a sirocco. Our way was still over a region of fine sand, spotted with shrubs, but all the traces of living things which had been so numerous the day before were effaced by the wind. We lunched at a place which seemed to promise a shelter, but even here the gale blew the sand in showers over our plates. A little beyond we passed a grove of palms in a hollow, on which the sand-hills were gaining; the trees on its western side were buried half way to their summits. Here were a few habitations of Bedouin Arabs, made of the long, stiff leaves of the palm stuck into the ground; and here was a well from which we made an addition to our supply of water. Further on, some enormous drifts of sand, loose, almost white, and bare of vegetation, approached the way. A camel lay dead in our path, and ravens were devouring it; they rose croaking as we came on, and flew aside. A mile further on was another camel, the bones of which were almost picked clean by the jackals and birds of prey. The wind became hotter and drier as we proceeded, keeping the sand in motion like snow, though it did not often raise it as high as our faces while we sat on our camels. About half-past four we came to a kind of shallow valley, where the shrubs and other plants of the desert seemed most numerous, and here, as the camels were fatigued with their day's march, it was judged best to pass the night. The little donkey, too, seemed weary with walking so long in the deep sand, and the monkey, as soon as he was taken down from his perch, began to dig up the juicy sorrel, which he ate greedily.

As the sun was going down, the wind abated somewhat in violence, but our dragoman and his assistants took the precaution of heaping the sand about the canvas of our tents at its lower edge, by way of confining the sheets in their places and keeping out the air. As the darkness came on the gale rose again, and at ten o'clock blew with more strength than ever. We were all in bed, but I could not sleep, and lay listening to the perpetual flapping of our canvas, and the sand striking against it in showers. At one o'clock in the morning came a furious gust, and wrenched up the stakes of our tent from the sand, dragging its poles and sheets over us, breaking down the bedstead on which I lay, overturning one or two of the others, and carrying away with the tent our clothes, watches, and books. I felt the current of sand sweeping over me, and was on my feet in an instant, shouting to Balthas and his assistants, who immediately came with lanterns. While they were struggling to raise our tent, their own was struck by a second gust, and laid even with the ground. After much effort the two tents were raised again and firmly secured with stakes and ropes. We groped in the sand for our stray watches, penknives, and other articles of value, which we recovered with little difficulty. My bed was made up again, on the carpet which floored our tent, and I had a nap of about three hours in sheets powdered with sand. The accident I have related happened on the morning of the fifth of February, the windiest and the warmest morning I had known in Egppt.

As we were taking down our tents the next morning, a centipede was found under ours—a frightful insect, with a multitude of legs and feelers, which has the reputation of being venomous. With considerable difficulty, our dragoman got it into a bottle of spirits, for it curled itself back from the mouth of the bottle again and again, and made a thousand efforts to escape the fate destined for it. A smaller one was found the evening before, running on the bedstead of one of our party.

The Arab who had taken away his camel on the morning of the day before, had returned in the evening, and assisted in raising our tents when they were blown down. At our request he was spared the flogging intended for him; his camel was loaded with the rest, and we set forward, intending to stop at Gatieh, a kind of oasis in the desert, once the seat of a considerable town, but now abandoned to the Bedouins. After a ride of two hours and a half, we saw its palms, towering at a distance, and passing to it over a plain thickly covered with shrubs, as it doubtless had once been with harvests, we set up our tents, at a little past mid-day, in a hollow shaded by a fine little grove of palms. The wind, though it was veering to a northerly direction, and had become cooler, still blew with considerable strength, and we made our tent-ropes fast to the trunks of the trees. The Arabs of the place came about us from a larger grove hard by, bringing fresh eggs and baskets for sale—children attracted by our monkey, which, tethered to a stake, was dancing backward and forward, and occasionally springing with his fiercest look toward the strangers who approached too near; and men, some of whom made a formidable appearance, with muskets slung on their shoulders. They complained, however, of the want of ammunition, and one of them offered to shoot a wild pig for us, if we would furnish him with powder. The offer was declined, but to let the Arabs know that we had powder enough for our own purposes, a gun was let off at a thievish-looking dog which came skulking about our encampment.

I could not but admire the grand looks of these brown people of the desert, the perfection of their forms, combining activity and strength, their well-formed features, eyes full of life, and white, even, undecayed teeth. The women wore on their foreheads and cheeks, a row of little circular plates of brass and coins, depending from a kind of cap, and the corners of their blue cotton mantles were sometimes neatly fastened together with a shell of the size of a pigeon's egg. I bought of them a little basket, handsomely wrought of a kind of rush, but before putting it into my travelling bag, I bethought me of a passage in Lane's account of the modern Egyptians. "Lice," says that minute and candid describer, "with the most scrupulous cleanliness, are not always to be avoided." I struck the basket lightly on a table, to see what might fall out of it, when one of the crawling nuisances made its appearance. I gave a smarter blow; two or three more followed, and I tossed the basket from me into a thicket of young palms.

LETTER X.

Seventh, eighth, and ninth days of our journey.—Bedouin huts.—Women at the hand-mills.—A salt-plain.—Ruins of a tower.—A well in the Desert.—Brackish water.—Arabs amusing themselves with our monkey.—Flocks of goats and sheep.—Importunity of the flies.—We meet a merchants' caravan.—Mosquitoes.—Animal life in the Desert.—Tracks of jackals and gazelles.—Sight of the Mediterranean.—Shrubs of the Desert.—Minute flowers.—Herd of camels feeding.—Pools of water in the salt-plains.—Springs of mineral oil.—Cry of the jackal.—Town of El Areesh.—Plantations of young palms.—Sand-hills and drifts.—Fruit-trees.

JERUSALEM, PALESTINE, February 22d, 1853.

WE went to look at the habitations of the Bedouins in a larger grove near us; they were huts made of the leaves of the date-palm, within little enclosures, formed by setting these leaves upright in the ground. We looked into one or two of these enclosures, where hand-mills were humming, and saw the women grinding millet. The quern they used was composed of two circular stones, with an iron handle on one side of the upper stone, and a raised border of dry mud and chopped straw on the lower, to prevent the escape of the meal. There were none but women and children about the dwellings. An old woman, tall, gaunt, and shrivelled, came up to us scowling, and accosted us in harsh, sharp tones, pointing in the direction of our encampment, and evidently ordering us away. A short old woman enforced the command in a milder voice, with the same gesture; so we bowed to the two ladies, and retired.

Close to this grove I saw the first instance of what travellers in the desert call a salt-plain. It was perfectly level, with a smooth, hard surface, bare of shrubs, except in a few hillocks, and wherever it was fully dry, white with a thin crust of salt. At the end next to the grove was a shallow pool of crystalline water, intensely salt, and near it several salt-wells, evidently deepened by human hands, full to the surface. We crossed the grove to the east side, where are the remains of the town destroyed by the French in their invasion of Egypt, under Bonaparte. They consist of mounds of earth, fragments of brick walls, and the tombs of two Santons—little Moslem chapels, with whitewashed domes. Not far from one of them grew an enormous tamarisk, with a thick head of boughs and foliage. Some of the richer portions of the ground were formed into little enclosures, with palm-branches set in the centre, where the Bedouins had cultivated their millet last year, and the rank weeds had just been plucked up to make room for another crop. Another grove of palms stood to the east of the ruins, and here in a little green hollow, where asses were feeding, were the remains of a higher antiquity—portions of a marble column or two, which had belonged to some temple of ancient Egyptian or Greek architecture.

In the afternoon our people repaired such of our furniture as had been broken by the accident of the night, and filled our water-cask from a broad, deep well lying in a hollow, to which we saw the young Bedouin women going along a well-beaten path, with jars on their heads. It was dug and lined with stone, by Mohammed Ali, while he was master of Syria, and provided with a spacious watering-trough of brick, covered with cement, for the camels of his military caravans. The water was brackish and unpalatable, but it was the best that could be had. We mounted our camels the next morning, amidst a throng of male and female Arabs, old and young, some diverting themselves with the monkey, and others clamoring for *bakhshish*. They pressed so near while the camels were loading, that our dragoman thought proper to flourish his cowskin over their heads. They scampered away to a little distance, laughing, and came back almost immediately. The clamors for *bakhshish* became louder as we began to move off, men and women lifted up their ragged children, and boys and girls held out their hands to us till we were fairly on our march.

We passed a shepherd of Gatieh driving a flock of about fifty sheep and goats toward a small palm-grove standing by itself, around which the shrubs grew more luxuriantly than elsewhere. The sheep were black, with coarse long wool, from which the Bedouins weave their cloaks and the sheets for their tents. Farther on we entered a hollow formed by heaps of sand, where were many shrubs and sometimes a little water. A swarm of flies came buzzing about us, insisting most perseveringly upon establishing themselves at the corners of our eyes. Diseased eyes are common among people of the poorer class in Egypt, and I never saw any effort made to drive away the flies that settle upon them. Children with a circle of flies around each eye are among the first things of which the traveller takes notice, and the grown-up Egyptian, accustomed to them by long habit, never thinks of brushing them off. It seems to me possible that the contagion of the ophthalmia, so prevalent in that country, may be propagated in this way.

Several camels appeared in sight. "It is a caravan," said one of our party, and so it proved. To meet a caravan in the desert, is an occasion of as much interest as to speak a vessel in a voyage from America to Europe. A train of ten camels was coming toward us in our path, loaded with large bales wrapped in coarse dark-brown woollen cloth, and bound with strong cords. On one of the camels sat the principal of the caravan, in his turban and gown, with a long gray beard and a long pipe, and a brace of pistols in his girdle. With him were seven other persons, some of whom were armed, three on the camels and four walking. Our dragoman stopped and conferred with the principal for a moment. "It is a merchants' caravan," said he, when we resumed our journey. "They are from Gaza, and are conveying silks and other merchandise of Syria to Cairo."

We did not think of being exposed to the persecutions of the mosquitoes in this arid region, but this day, as we were taking our lunch near a hollow where the sand had a moist appearance, they came about us, hungry and sharp-bitten, and with them a cloud of midges, or sand-flies, extremely troublesome. There were other living things of the desert with which we had now become familiar—sand-colored lizards, one kind slender and swift, which often shot across our path; another, clumsily shaped and slow, scarcely able to get out of the way of our camels; moths fluttering about the flowers of the desert, and here and there a butterfly; snails clinging to every shrub, and the surface for several feet around strewn with their white shells, now empty; land-tortoises creeping beside the way; sluggish chameleons, of which we took several; black-beetles, rolling along fresh balls of camel's dung; and snakes, of which we killed a small, spotted one, said by our Arabs to be venomous. Now and then a heron would rise from a pool of brackish water, where he sought his food, and ravens, on their glistening black wings, were always hovering near us.

Close to our path were the burrows of the jackal in the hillocks, and the marks of their feet in the sand, as well as those of the jerboa, or leaping rat, which has numerous holes all over the desert. Less frequently seen was the track of the gazelle, a delicate triangular foot-print. The skeletons of camels were scattered all along the way, where they had fallen and perished, for when the camel gives out under his load, his owner knows that his end is come, and leaves him to die. In a night or two, nothing is left of him but the bones.

It was a fine, cool day, with a bracing north-westerly wind. The sky, which during the sirocco that overturned our tent had been filled with a thick, white haze, from the fine particles of sand, blown up and suspended by the force of the wind, had become perfectly transparent, and the currents of air passing through it came to us directly from the Mediterranean. In ascending a bank, we had the sea before us—the solitary sea—murmuring along a vast extent of uninhabited shore. That night we pitched our tent in a wide plain, with a steep, low bank on the south, beside which the rain-water gathers in the winter, and forms a kind of marsh. The mosquitoes came swarming into our tent, and unlike any of their tribe we had seen before, plunged into the flame of our candles. We made the tent-door fast, and in a short time the greater part of them had singed their wings, and were heaped about the foot of the candles, so that we were little disturbed by them during the night.

The morning of the 7th of February was chilly with the air from the sea, and we were later than usual in leaving our encampment. A journey of an hour and a half over heavy sand brought us to another of the salt-plains I have mentioned, perfectly level, hard under foot, with large patches of a bare smooth surface. In other places it was covered with a growth of bushes. Beyond, we entered upon a winding hollow, looking almost like a regular highway, with many shrubs on the left hand, from which rose myriads of mosquitoes and midges, bred by the recent rains. Of the shrubs of the desert nearly all are evergreens; some are thorny, but the greater number are of a jointed growth, somewhat like the rush, in the younger or greener stems of which the moisture imbibed from the soil during winter is secreted and preserved in store for the dry season, supplying a juicy pasturage for the camels. Among these shrubs the *retem*, or broom of the desert, is one of the most conspicuous as well as the most beautiful, bearing a profusion of white flowers veined with purple. The shrubs send their roots far into the loose soil in search of moisture, and the sand being heaped about them by the winds, they form hillocks, held in shape by a net-work of roots, in which the jackal and jerboa have their habitations. The ground in many places at this season was starred with a multitude of little flowers—a small pink phlox, a plant of the geranium family, with a purple bloom; another of the mustard family, of a delicate white; and several compound flowers, both white and yellow, some of them fragrant, all dwarfed by the meagre soil, but making the banks gay under the shrubs. The scarlet poppy showed itself to-day, in little groups on a declivity beside our path.

In our journey this morning several camels appeared in sight, which at first we thought to be a caravan. As we came nearer, camel after camel was seen, a numerous troop, scattered over a considerable space, browsing among the bushes and herbage. They were the property of the Bedouins, feeding in the broad pasture of their owners, the desert. Further on we descended into an oval salt-plain lying among drifts of sand, with a surface as even as a mirror, and wholly bare.of vegetation except at the edges to the right and left of our way. A winding path among sand-hills led us from this to another, and in this manner we traversed, in the course of the day, four salt-plains, one of which in the direction we were travelling, we computed to be at least a mile and a half across, and in two of which were shallow pools of water, intensely salt, clear and colorless, and sparkling as they were rippled by the wind. On coming to these plains we immediately dismounted and walked; it was a luxury, after riding through drifts of sand, to tread a surface so firm and even. We followed a path made by the broad and heavy foot-prints of the camel, but this was crossed by the tracks of the gazelle and the jackal in all directions.

On climbing out of these plains we had glimpses of the Mediterranean to the north of us, and salt-pools in the hollows between us and the sea. To the southeast rose the varied peaks of a range of mountains lying along the shore of the Red Sea. When I was in Upper Egypt, I fell in with an Italian who was employed to obtain sulphur from a mine among these mountains. "They are incredibly rich," said he, "in beds of ore of various metals and other mineral productions; but these cannot be worked for want of fuel. Egypt has no mines of coal; all that is used in her steamers and her manufactures, is brought from England. She has springs of mineral oil, the indication of beds of coal, and wherever they are to be found, the government has made excavations to a great depth, and at great cost, but without success. An Arab in wandering among the mountains near the Red Sea, not long since, found a little pool of quicksilver, where it had flowed from the rocks. He attempted to scoop it up with his hands, but it slid through his fingers; he then drew it up into his mouth, filled with it the leathern bottle in which he carried water, and brought it home. He was taken ill immediately afterward and died, probably from the effect of the quicksilver he had swallowed, so that the spot where he found it is still unknown, though diligent search has been made for it."

We stopped for the night as usual, in a hollow, where we might be sheltered from the wind, and toward morning I heard the cry of the jackals for the first time, though for several nights they had been our neighbors. They were answered by our donkey with a gallant bray, after which I heard them no more. This was succeeded, as the day dawned, by a more welcome song, the cheerful twittering of birds about our tent. The morning was clear and cold; the weak herbs of the desert were flattened to the earth beneath a load of dew; and as we were taking our breakfast in the open air at sunrise, a troop of small birds, apparently of the sparrow family, were busy about us, gathering their early meal on our camping-ground.

This day, the 8th of February, was to bring us to the lonely little town of El Areesh, on the shore of the sea. As we approached it, we observed that our path became more like a beaten highway, and the region better suited to pasturage. We passed a large herd of young camels belonging to the people of El Areesh, feeding under a steep bank, at the foot of which the shrubs were more numerous and the herbage greener than elsewhere. We lunched in a little salt-plain, in the neighborhood of which the declivities seemed on flame with scarlet poppies, and a liliaceous flower on a long stalk made its appearance among the shrubs. Within about three miles of El Areesh, we heard a chorus of shrill cries, and saw grazing in a deep circular basin of a few rods over, covered at the bottom and sides with luxuriant herbage of the liveliest green, a dozen or more camels, wearing the rude wooden frames which serve as saddles, and tended by boys. We now overtook women driving home donkeys loaded with brushwood gathered in the desert, and camels almost hidden under enormous piles of coarse hay, made of a grass which grows in large solitary tufts. Here and there stood a cluster of palms in a hollow, and in some places little plantations of the young tree were formed, with circular depressions about the stem, to receive the water necessary to keep them from perishing.

To the left of our path, on the side next to the

sea, were banks of freshly drifted sand, with towering crests, and among these we at length entered by a deep hollow path, within which the rays of the sun beat upon us with sickening force. Climbing out of it by a steep ascent, we came upon a dreary waste utterly without vegetation, where the arid wind sifted the sand and piled it in broad hills all around us. In all my journey I had seen no aspect of nature so melancholy as that on which I now looked. With every wind from the west or the northwest, these enormous drifts, elevated above the surrounding region, must continue to extend themselves, burying all vegetable growth far below their surface, and carrying with them the desolation which everywhere met my eyes. We followed a broad track, like one made over fresh-fallen snow, and which the next wind must efface, for nearly two miles, amidst a crowd of people returning from the desert. At length the walls of the fortress of El Areesh, built by the French in the time of the Directory, were before us. The drifts had reached the foot of its western wall, covering the site of former habitations, traces of which were yet visible, and half burying one or two structures of stone which had been abandoned. The town is a little collection of huts, within the walls of the fortress, and on its eastern side. The inhabitants subsist by rearing camels, which find a broad range and abundant pasturage in the neighboring desert.

The Arabs of our party were all inhabitants of El Areesh; their friends came about us to help them unload their camels, and our tents were soon pitched on the edge of the loose sands, to the south of the fortress. Meantime we strolled into the town, which presented the usual aspect of the Arab villages we had seen—rows of low flat-roofed houses built of mud, put into the shape of brick—narrow streets, filth, and people asking alms. In that part of the town which lay east of the fortress was a well, with a large wheel for raising its brackish water, which the people of the place, who had probably never tasted any better, assured us was excellent. A little eastward of the village stood a small building of stone, with four open arches on the sides. It covered a broad, deep well, regularly lined with hewn stone, from which the neighboring fields might have been irrigated a hundred years ago, but it was now dry. At a little distance to the southwest of our encampment was an enclosure of fruit-trees, the fig and apricot, protected by a wall; the hills of sand were already peeping over it, and had invaded one corner, threatening to overwhelm the whole in a short time.

LETTER XI.

Tenth day of the journey.—Picturesque costumes.—Spirited horses and horsemanship.—Trouble with passports.—Barley-fields.—Women cutting up juniper.—Tributes to the Arabs.—An Arab exquisite.—A pastoral region.—Another tribute.—A salt lake.—Safayda.—Tomb of a Santon.—Flocks of birds.—Frightful scream of a jackal.—Reading the Scriptures.—A troop of dervishes.—An Arab cemetery.

JERUSALEM, PALESTINE, February 22d, 1853.

NEXT morning, as we were striking our tents and loading our camels, we were surrounded by a large circle of admiring spectators, men, women, and children, who came to see the Franks and the monkey. "Thieves, all," said the father of couriers—I believe he slandered them—" every one of them thieves," and drawing his short sword, the first time he had employed it in our defence, he rushed among them with a terrific shout and dispersed them. In the mean time, a little party of cavalry belonging to the detachment which we had seen leaving Belbays, rode up to the fortress, from their camp in a palm-grove, north of the town, on the sea-shore. We could not but admire their picturesque costume, so gracefully worn; that of each individual differing in some respect of color or arrangement from those of all the rest. Some had muskets slung on their backs, one or two carried theirs on their shoulders, with the butt behind them, and one bore the black ensign of the Egyptian cavalry. They rode spirited and well-trained horses, which they managed with perfect ease, galloping swiftly to and fro, and stopping or wheeling them in mid-speed. I have seen nothing more showy and striking in all the East, and scarce anywhere else, than the spectacle of one of these horsemen, armed and arrayed in the Oriental fashion, and managing his horse in the Oriental manner. The government here is beginning to put its soldiers into a clumsy uniform of jacket and pantaloons, in which they make an insignificant appearance.

El Areesh is the frontier town of the dominions of the Egyptian Viceroy. Two men came early in the morning for our passports, telling us that they would be examined, and returned in a few minutes. We were ready to depart, and they had not arrived; we sent our dragoman to demand them. In the mean time we had leisure to observe the people who gathered about us. The peculiarities of the Egyptian physiognomy, which give it a resemblance to the faces sculptured in the old hieroglyphics, had entirely disappeared. Some of the men had fine persons and majestic beards, and a few light hair and gray or blue eyes.

Our dragoman returned with the passports in about an hour. Ten minutes would have sufficed to examine and countersign them, but the governor of the place, a lazy Turk, declared that he would not look at them till he had his coffee. When he had got his coffee, he declared that he would not attend to any business till he had finished his pipe. After smoking till he had brought himself to a more complying humor, he wrote two or three words in Arabic on each of the passports, and handed them to our messenger.

We set forward about half-past nine o'clock, amidst flocks of sheep and goats, with a few camels and asses which the herdsmen of El Areesh were driving afield. The region immediately east of the town had the appearance of being susceptible of cultivation, and here and there we saw patches of barley which showed that the soil was not naturally unfruitful. Crossing a dry water-course, about a mile and a half from the town, we entered a tract of pasturage and bushes where women were cutting up with mattocks an evergreen shrub, apparently a sort of heath, which they used to heat their ovens. In an Arab household, it is the goodwife whose business it is to provide the fuel. A troop of women, barefoot, in the usual loose dress of blue cotton, passed us, bearing bundles of this brushwood on their heads, and looking at us shyly from under the mantles which they drew over the lower part of their faces. The country here was full of flocks, each tended separately by its keepers, men or women; and in the more fertile places were little fields of springing barley.

At a distance of three or four miles from El Areesh, we entered upon a territory possessed by the race of Arabs who dwell in tents. Here the traveller pays a fixed tribute, which has the sanction of the government, to the sheikhs, in consideration of which they engage to protect him against robberies within their respective districts; in other words, they accept the tribute as a compensation for the robberies they would otherwise commit. Our dragoman was to pay these tributes, among the other expenses of our journey.

Two men, one on foot and the other on horseback, were seen coming over an eminence to the east of our path; our dragoman stopped, held a spirited parley in Arabic with the one on foot, and ended by giving him money. I was much struck with the showy costume of this chief, and quite as much with a certain grim beauty in his aspect. He wore a snowy white turban, a long white shirt with a red tunic over it, a sabre by his side, and thrown over one shoulder an Arab cloak, with broad stripes of white and black. His person was thin and sinewy, his features regular, with a jetty beard, a keen restless eye, and two rows of even, glittering teeth, that were visible to the very corners of his mouth at the least motion of his lips. His companion, who was scarcely less showily arrayed, was an elder and graver man; he wore a sabre and carried a long pipe, which he smoked during the conference. I asked our dragoman what was the subject of the dispute.

"The tribute allowed by the government," he

replied, "is three piastres for each traveller; the servants pay nothing. That sheikh insisted on having three piastres from each of us, with the exception of our four Arabs. I paid him twelve piastres for our four travellers, and three more for *bakhshish*. He knew he was not entitled to any more, for he thanked me and wished us a good journey."

The country now wore a pastoral look; on each side of our way were flocks tended by groups of men and women, whose voices are often heard before they are in sight. The herbage became more abundant as we went on, and the flowers larger, but everywhere the verdure was overlooked by a range of smooth hills of sand on our left, threatening to overwhelm us. We took our lunch in a salt-plain, from which we entered on a long, narrow, green vale, fragrant with a yellow flower of a plant called by our dragoman the wild camomile. I was walking on with two of my companions, when we saw before us, sitting on a bank by the path, four men, two of them armed with muskets, who were soon joined by a fifth. They were the collectors of the revenue for the sheikh of a new district. We saluted them and passed on, but they stopped our caravan as it came up; another parley was held, and another tribute of twelve piastres paid.

We walked on through a flock of sheep and goats feeding on both sides of our way, tended by women, who ran away at our approach; all but one slender brown maiden, who kept watch of her charge and us from a neighboring bank. We stopped to observe the beauty of the animals, which had a well-fed appearance. The goats were black, with long, wavy hair, which glistened like silk in the sunshine. The sheep, many of which were young, and had not yet parted with their first fleece, were beautifully marked; they had black feet, coal-black heads for the most part, and fleeces of clean white, with broad spots of raven black. As we stood looking at them, the maiden stretched her little brown neck above the shrubs, as if she were not perfectly sure whether we were not making our choice of the best of her flock.

After we had again mounted our camels, we came to a sandy ridge crossing our path, close by which stood a young Arab, of placid features, who seemed to be waiting for us. We stopped, and after a moment's conversation the young fellow was joined by a tall, thin black man, a Nubian, as they call them here, wearing a white turban, a long white shirt, and a sabre, who took up the discourse and spoke with much energy and gesticulation. Here was another demand for tribute. Twelve piastres were put into the palm of the negro, who handed them over to the Arab, the sheikh of the district, or the sheikh's son.

As we went on, Arabs and their animals were seen everywhere around us, but nowhere a trace of human habitation. Larger tracts of land under tillage appeared than we had before seen in the desert, some green with barley, others just ploughed, others lying fallow. At length our road ran for a short distance along the banks of a clear little lake. I dismounted and tasted its waters; they were as salt as the ocean. To the north of this lake was a smooth round hill of sand, evidently advancing into it, and there, half buried by the drifts, stood a little grove of palms. To the east of the lake was a salt-plain, into which we passed, ending in smooth slopes, clothed with short herbage, where cows, sheep, and camels, tended by Arabs, were grazing.

Here were the walls of a few ruined cottages, a cemetery beyond them, in which stood a *wely*, or tomb of a Mohammedan saint, with a whitewashed dome, and near the cemetery a few palm-trees.

"This place," said our dragoman, "is called Safzayda, and here we stop for the night. A few years ago there was a village on this spot, and in former times, I am told, a considerable town." Our people immediately began to unload the camels and to pitch our tents in the midst of the flocks, while I strolled toward the cemetery.

Within the tomb of the saint was a rude sarcophagus of stone, plastered over with mortar, and covered with a faded green cloth. Above it was stretched a cord, on which were strung bits of cloth, shells, and little frames of wood and paper stained with various colors, which I afterward learned were suspended there by persons afflicted with diseases, in the belief that there was a virtue in the tomb of a holy man which would work a cure. A marble slab, at the door of the tomb, bore a long Arabic inscription, the only one in all that place. The tombs around were numerous, formed of small stones covered with coarse mortar, but the more recent graves merely had loose stones piled over them, or were heaped with earth. The Bedouins had made this their burial-place.

The sun was now setting; women, in blue gowns, and shrill-voiced boys, were running about, hastily gathering their herds and flocks, and driving them over the hill to the south of us till the last of them had disappeared; thousands of small birds, keeping up an incessant twittering, were settling on the palms about us, their perch for the night, till the rigid branches bent with their weight. I returned to our tent, where our Arabs had collected brushwood and had kindled a fire, by which they were to keep watch during the night against the Bedouins and the jackals. At El Areesh we had left behind our donkey, which had grown thin with wading through the sand, and had re-enforced our caravan with two more Arabs, one of whom, a young fellow, rode one of the camels, and the other, a stout-legged man, armed with a brace of pistols, which he carried in his gay-colored sash, walked with the rest. The young man had made a luxurious bed on the ground with mats and quilts, but the other was preparing to pass the night with the camel-drivers.

One of the entertainments of our journey through the desert was reading books of travels relating to the country through which we were passing. Sometimes as we sat on our camels one would read aloud for the benefit of the rest, and in the evening, before we became drowsy, which was early enough, a little time was generally employed in this way. For these evening readings we frequently took parts of the Scriptures, to which the scenes around us gave a new interest —narratives of the journeys of the early Hebrews to the land of Egypt. Their abode in the country, their passage out of it, and wanderings in the desert, which once brought them to the very region in which we were travelling. This evening, while we were thus engaged, we were startled by loud cries, close to our tent, and almost in our ears. The sounds had in them something frightfully human. "It is a jackal," said one of the attendants. The animal had come prowling about our tent, but must have been scared away immediately, for we afterward heard the same cries from a distance.

Next morning, soon after sunrise, I went to the top of the hill which lay south of us, but nowhere could I descry the habitations of the Arabs, though we had heard their dogs answering the jackals all night. I returned to our encampment, where, as we were at breakfast, we observed a troop of ten men on foot approaching by the road we had travelled the day before. About half their number wore high, shaggy woollen caps, of a brown color, the costume of the dervishes, and two of them carried on their backs loads of dry brushwood. They halted at a little distance from us, sat down in a circle on the ground, and sent one of the wearers of the shaggy caps to borrow a live coal or two from our cook's fire. We learned from him that this was a troop of holy men, pilgrims from Persia and Bokhara, who had been to Mecca, and were now on their way to the holy places in Syria. The dervish was a good-natured looking fellow, with a pair of blinking eyes, ragged, barefooted, and fat. He returned to his companions, and probably made a report to them of what he saw on our breakfast-table, for immediately another deputation was sent, asking for something to eat.

Our dragoman, thrifty in his charity, gave them two loaves of bread, brought from Cairo, which had begun to be a little mouldy.

While our camels were loading, I walked again to the Arab burial-place. Even in this desert is felt the instinct which prompts us to beautify the resting-places of the dead. The region produces a liliaceous plant, with a large bulb and large thick leaves of a deep-green color. Bunches of these were planted at the head and foot of many of the graves. A singular custom, I perceived, prevails here, of laying the garments of the dead on the ground above them. At the head of one of the graves lay a woman's blue cotton dress, as fresh, almost, in appearance, as if it had just come from the loom. I remarked several articles of male attire, some of them much decayed by the length of time they had remained on the ground. On one poor fellow's grave lay only his thrum-cap, probably the sole part of his raiment which was thought in a fit condition to serve as his monument. The grave of a child fixed my attention, at each end of which a tuft of the plant I have already mentioned was growing freshly, and between them lay a little garment of blue cotton, and another of white, with a crimson stripe running through it. Near by, and probably dragged away by the jackals, was the skin of a lamb, with a soft silky fleece, which had formed the child's outer garment in winter. I replaced it on the grave, and could not help thinking how tenderly, to judge by these tokens, that child must have been cherished, and that, when it was carried out dead from the humble abode of its parents, their low brown tent pitched on the greensward, the heart of its mother must have been pierced by a sorrow as sharp as is felt at such a loss in the most civilized country.

LETTER XII.

Cultivated fields between bare sand-hills.—Ruins of Rhaphia.—The virgin's fountain.—Khan Yoonas.—Fruit-trees in bloom.—Our party in quarantine.—We pass the night in a cemetery.—A crowd of women in white, among the graves.—Oranges.—Distinguished-looking visitors.—Departure from Khan Yoonas.—Pilgrims.—The scarlet anemone.—Old sycamores.—Men ploughing with camels.—We enter the lazaretto at Gaza.—View of the country from our windows.—Foolish look of the dervishes.—Our monkey attacks one of the holy men.—An Arab virago.—Show of tongues.—Release from the lazaretto.

JERUSALEM, PALESTINE, February 22d, 1853.

It was a cool morning, and on leaving Safzayda, I walked on before the caravan, with two of my companions, in a long valley, between cultivated fields on each side of the way for a considerable distance, in the midst of which a broad irregular stripe of greensward and shrubs was left for travellers. Arab men and women appeared from time to time on the heights with their sheep and camels, and groups of women were chattering in the road before us, who took good care to be out of our way as we approached. The long line of bare sand-hills which border the sea continued in sight to the northwest, and once we had a view of the Mediterranean over it. Not long afterward we came to a region of pasturage, where the ground was covered with short herbage, consisting principally of a kind of trefoil, with very minute leaves, and here, in a shallow vale, sheltered on the east and north, and opening to the southwest, lay the dark brown tents of the Bedouins, made of a coarse cloth, woven from the fleeces of their sheep. Cows, sheep, goats, and camels were grazing about us, and from the tents the whooping of children was heard.

On the right of our path, at a little distance before us, appeared a mound, on which stood two columns, their pedestals buried in the earth, which was full of bits of marble and fragments of pottery. Here was the site óf Rhaphia, once a populous city. "These columns," said the dragoman, "belonged to a Greek church, built where the Virgin rested in her flight to Egypt, and you will see more of them a little further on, in a place where we shall take our lunch. There is a fountain of sweet water there, which came out of the ground by a miracle, to quench the Virgin's thirst." We descended from the mound into a hollow, where this miraculous fountain was. It was a deep well, with a very little water in it, around which lay scattered several marble columns, and broken pedestals of columns. The herbage was here luxuriant, and our camels cropped it eagerly.

At a little past two o'clock on that day, the 10th of February, we found ourselves among the gardens of Khan Yoonas, the frontier town of Syria. They were hedged with rows of the prickly pear, and full of almond, peach, and apricot trees, in full bloom, with here and there a tamarisk and sycamore next to the way. Just at the entrance of the town, which is a wretched one, we were conducted into an enclosure serving as a lazaretto, surrounded by a fence formed by the branches of a thorny tree, called the *nebek*, set upright in the ground—and were informed that we were in quarantine. Part of a Turkish cemetery had been taken into the lazaretto, and we pitched our tents and spread our carpets on the old neglected graves. In that part of the cemetery which lay without were more than fifty women, nearly all in white, with long white mantles covering the head and reaching nearly down to the feet, sitting around the graves or moving silently among them like ghosts. "They are mourning for the dead," said Vincenzo.

Our new acquaintances, the pilgrims, two or three of them bearing a load of brushwood, entered the enclosure along with us and squatted down in one corner. In another part a company of Arabs, men, women, and children, had established themselves; the men, after taking their midday meal, rolled themselves in their cloaks, covering their heads from sight, and lay asleep on the ground. The keepers of the quarantine had a hut of dry reeds and boughs within the lazaretto, before which they were posted with clubs and boughs of trees, to keep the travellers from going out, and from coming too near the people of the place when they entered the lazaretto. One of our caravan bought some oranges of one of the keepers. He threw a piastre toward the keeper, who poured a pitcher of water over it as it lay on the ground, to purify it from the contagion we were supposed to bring from Egypt, and then taking it up, tossed back four oranges.

Next morning, before sunrise, the pilgrims were heard chanting their prayers. While we were breakfasting and loading our camels, three men, of a remarkably striking appearance, entered the lazaretto, and after standing awhile to observe us, sat down on a mat before the hut, and watched our proceedings at their leisure. One of them, in a snowy-white turban, had a beard as white, and was wrapped in an ample black gown; another, of tall stature and lofty air, in a costume of intermingled white, red, and yellow, wore red morocco boots and a sabre with a glittering handle and scabbard; the third, younger than either, had on the amplest and whitest of oriental petticoats. About eight o'clock, a man on a spirited horse, and wearing a sabre, presented himself at the entrance of the lazaretto; it was our guardian who was to accompany us to Gaza. The term of quarantine performed by travellers arriving in Syria from Egypt is five days. The day on which they arrive at Khan Yoonas, if they enter the lazaretto before sunset, is counted as the first; the day passed in travelling from Khan Yoonas to Gaza is the second; two days and three nights are then passed in the lazaretto at Gaza, and the day on the morning of which they leave the lazaretto completes the five.

At half-past eight we left the lazaretto under

the conduct of our guardian—a long train of Franks, pilgrims, Arab men, women, and children, camels, and asses. Of the children, eight or nine in number, some were put on the donkeys, others were carried by their parents, and our good-natured Arabs gave a woman and her baby a seat on one of their camels. One of the donkeys trotted along under a cluster of three children, clinging to each other, the eldest of whom, not more than eight years old, guided the animal. We had left the desert, and now entered on a grassy plain with a range of sand-hills on its western boundary, and verdant eminences to the east. It was gaudy with yellow flowers, and in some places red with the scarlet anemone, and over it were scattered, at considerable distances from each other, sycamores centuries old, with enormous gnarled and twisted trunks. Our pilgrims, as they marched before us, sang in chorus one of their hymns, the sound of which came to us on the wind.

Two or three miles north of Khan Yoonas appeared, far to the east, a cluster of the dark tents of the Bedouins, with smoke rising from them. They were probably inhabited by the keepers of the flocks which were feeding near our path, and which our guardian, with drawn sabre, chased out of our way, lest peradventure we should give them the plague. As the people of the country met us, the cry of *carantina, carantina!* was raised, and they turned to the right or the left, allowing us a broad passage over the plain.

As we approached Gaza, the number of trees diminished, and the tilled fields became more numerous. We saw people ploughing with camels; the ploughs were of wood, light, and with a slender upright handle; the wooden share merely scratched the surface of the ground. At length we came in sight of the minarets of Gaza, situated amidst gardens and trees and gentle eminences. The guardian made our whole train enter the lazaretto, an enclosure with high walls, just at the entrance of the town, having a large well in the midst, and a long low building near the side, opposite to the entrance. At each end of this building was a second story, consisting of two small chambers, one set of which was assigned to us, while our dragoman and his people occupied a room below.

It was now one o'clock in the afternoon, and

we had the rest of the day and two days more to pass in the lazaretto. We did not find our imprisonment so tedious as we expected. We read, we wrote, we paced the wall at our end of the lazaretto; we looked at the surrounding country from our windows; a green, treeless plain to the south; and to the north a region rising into pleasant slopes, covered with trees, mostly the olive, among which stood the flat-roofed buildings of the town and its towering minarets. Over this scene were sweeping the shadows of clouds brought by a cool wind from the sea. We observed the women of the place washing clothes at a little sheet of water at the east of us, almost under the walls of the lazaretto, or sitting on the grass in their long white mantles, with their children playing beside them. We watched our friends, the dervishes and pilgrims, at their devotions, prostrating themselves on their faces from time to time, in their prayers, which they uttered inaudibly, with moving lips. These holy men had their time fully occupied with prayers, sleeping in the sun, and picking the vermin—the lice, if you must have the word —from the inside of their garments, which they took off and carefully examined once a day at least, during their stay in the lazaretto. Five of the party, we now learned, were regular dervishes; the others, ordinary pilgrims. The dervishes were particularly ragged, with patched garments of many colors; but they looked well-fed, and had a foolish expression of face. The only man among them who was not ragged was one of the ordinary pilgrims, a lean fellow, with an anxious look, who wore a sabre by his side. The dervishes manifested a great desire to amuse themselves with our monkey, after an example which we had set them; but the creature, though tolerably well-behaved toward our party, would endure no familiarities from strangers. He was fastened by a long cord to the iron grate of our dragoman's window, but whenever the dervishes approached him, he sprung at them into the air, with his fiercest grin, and tore their rags and their sacred skins without mercy. We saw the blood trickling down the plump, swarthy leg of the principal dervish of the party, after a brief interview with the monkey.

Among those who entered the lazaretto with us was an Arab family with several children, the mother of which was endowed with a shrill voice and a most voluble tongue. She was in constant dispute with one of the keepers, who brought us bread from the town, and who insisted upon having his profit on every loaf. For this the woman attacked him whenever he appeared, with reproaches, uttered in the most rapid Arabic. To do him justice, he stood his ground bravely, and answered like one who was practised in such quarrels, but after they had shouted and gesticulated at each other for a quarter of an hour, he generally gave in and retreated, the woman screaming after him as he went. One of our party hearing the cause of her complaint, gave her a few Turkish coins to buy bread for her children. This brought upon him a torrent of thanks and blessings, and it was observed that the disputes of the woman with the keeper were carried on with less animation.

On the third day after we entered the lazaretto, a little before sunset, a message was brought us from the physician, desiring that we would do him the favor to come down stairs. We descended to the court of the lazaretto, and stood in a row before Dr. Eperon, a slender

Frenchman of, perhaps, thirty years of age, who planted himself at a safe distance from us, and politely asked us in his native language if we were quite well.

"Perfectly so," was our answer.

"I am glad of it," said the doctor; "but you must excuse me if I go through with certain formalities. Will you be so kind as to let me see your tongues?"

We all put out our tongues together.

"That will do," said he; "to-morrow morning, after sunrise, you are at liberty to leave the lazaretto." We bowed and returned to our rooms, whither we were followed by one of the keepers, who brought a brazier full of live coals, and throwing into it a small quantity of sulphur, fumigated our persons and our clothes.

LETTER XIII.

Continuation of the journey to Jerusalem.—The Gate of Gaza.—A vast olive-grove.—Curious travelling cradle.—Remains of a Christian church.—Askelon.—Ancient walls.—Sand drifting over the fields.—El Medjal.—Little oxen.—Rude ploughs.—Ashdod.—Ruins of a large Khan.—A chorus of frogs.—Gazelles feeding.—Village of Zebua.—Saracenic bridges.—Women carrying burdens.—Town of Ramleh.—An abandoned tower.—Plain of Sharon.—A convent, where we pass the night.—The mosquitoes from the cisterns.

JERUSALEM, PALESTINE, February 22d, 1853.

ON leaving the lazaretto next morning, our dragoman took us through a part of the dirty town, to show us some things which, he said, were always visited by travellers. He stopped us at a remnant of an old wall, on the side of which was seen the beginning of an arch that had once, apparently, extended over the way. "This," said he, "is the gate of Gaza, the doors of which were carried away by Samson. There," pointing to some granite columns lying on the ground, "are part of the temple which Samson pulled down upon the heads of the Philistines." We did not linger long to look at these apocryphal antiquities, but went on through the vast olive-grove lying north of the town, a monument of past ages, concerning which there could be no doubt. It fills the whole breadth of the valley, from east to west, and extends northward to the distance of about four miles. The trees are old and venerable, with enormous stems of an irregular growth, and on that morning the sunshine came down pleasantly among them upon the verdure, which was sprinkled with flowers. We met many of the people of the neighborhood in their picturesque oriental costume, coming into town; some of them driving asses loaded with green crops, freshly gathered. On one of these animals a cradle, made for carrying an infant, was swinging, supported by two upright posts, fastened to the sides of the saddle, in which the little traveller might ride as much at his ease as in the arms of his mother.

Our dragoman had promised to show us the ruins of Askelon. He took us across a spur of the sand-hills, that border the sea, a waste in which, to judge from the huge sycamores still scattered over it, harvests had once been gathered, and descending into a little green vale planted with olive-trees, led us again up the banks of sand, and finally brought us to the remains of a massive wall, with a broad arched door, about a quarter of a mile from the seashore. "These," said he, "are the remains of a Christian church of the City of Askelon. The columns belonging to this church were dragged to the sea and thrown into it, when the city was destroyed, and its port filled up." The loose sands had drifted about the spot where we stood. Between us and the shore were other remains—portions of ancient walls and fortifications, against which the sand was heaped, and the waves of the sea were breaking on fragments of old quays, now wholly deserted. Only in a little valley to the northeast, green with herbage, and planted with fruit-trees, stood a cluster of mud cottages; all that is left of that great commercial city for which the east and the west contended so fiercely for so many centuries.

From this scene of desolation we turned away, and descending the sand-hills where the wind has piled them about the olive-trees almost to their upper branches, we came to green meadows, with pools of rain-water lying among them, overlooked by the little town of El Medjal. It is pleasantly situated on a bank, with tall minarets rising above its trees. Fortunately, our road did not pass through it, so there was nothing to mar the agreeable impression made by the beauty of its aspect at a little distance. Beyond, the peasants were ploughing their fields with light ploughs, drawn by little oxen, of a size, which in our country, would make them pass for steers of two years old. One hand held the upright handle of the plough, and the other guided the oxen. The shares, as they traced a shallow furrow, uprooted tufts of narcissus in bloom.

When at length we overtook our loaded camels, they had stopped for the night on a tract of pasturage, where herds and flocks were feeding, and a pool of fresh water lay beside the ridge of sand-hills. At a little distance was the town of Esdud, the Ashdod of the Philistines and the Azotus of later times, seated on a little eminence, not far from which lay the ruins of a spacious khan or caravanserai. As the sun was going down, the women and boys of the village came about us, collecting the sheep and cattle, and driving them to their folds for the night, and laborers, one after another, passed us, returning from the fields, with donkeys bearing their ploughs, harrows, and mattocks—for no vehicle on wheels, even of the humblest kind, is ever seen in any part of Syria.

It was a luxury to dine again in our tent, unmolested by flies, which swarmed in the lazaretto we had left; and, at a later hour, to stretch our limbs on our beds, sure that our slumbers would not be disturbed by fleas, with which the lazaretto was alive in every part. There was a hoarse chorus of frogs from the pool, but this mingling with the roar of the Mediterranean as it broke on the sand-hills to the west of our encampment, was really sleep-inspiring. In the morning, while our camels were getting ready, we visited the ruins of the khan. Massive piers of hewn stone, six feet in diameter, uphold a row of pointed Saracenic arches, surrounding a quadrangle of a hundred and fifty feet square, the pavement of which yet remains. Here are the vaults, some of them yet entire, in which travellers and merchants once stabled camels, or had their merchandise locked up for the night; and traces of the hinges are yet seen upon which the huge gates of the place were turned. The khan in these parts seems once to have served not only as a place of shelter, but as a stronghold, in which the caravans were safe against surprises by night.

We walked up to the town, from which we had a view of the surrounding country. A broad, shallow basin lay before us, green, treeless, fenceless, uninhabited, like the prairies of the West. Along the bottom of this vale we followed a path leading almost due north, among extensive fields of grain and wastes of pasturage. About noon, one of our train pointed to the declivities on the eastern side, and said: "There are gazelles feeding." We looked, and saw twelve of these beautiful creatures, quietly grazing on the green slope, seven in one troop and five in another. Immediately Balthas was on the ground, with his rifle, in pursuit of them. They took the alarm, and began to move off slowly; he fired while yet at too great a distance for any certain aim, and the instant the smoke broke from the muzzle, they were in full flight, bounding airily away to the southeast, till they were out of sight. I should have hardly thought it possible for fear to manifest itself so gracefully.

Our caravan made its halt at noon, on a green near the village of Zebna, where, as we sat on the grass, we had before us a fine broad valley; the village, with a square tower in the midst, seated on a little hill, and beyond it the dark range of the mountains of Judea. Going up to the village, we found the tower to belong to what was once a Christian church, now used for a school, built, as was manifest from its architecture, in the time of the Crusaders, who have left the tokens of their occupation scattered through the country. Part of the walls had fallen, leaving the building open on one side, but the rest, with its pointed arches, was in perfect preservation. There was nobody in or about the building, but the space within had been carefully and neatly swept; perhaps it had served as a school that morning.

Both beyond Zebna, and before arriving at it, we crossed several Saracenic bridges over small streams, vestiges of the dominion of a race as energetic as the Crusaders, and in their day, perhaps, considerably more civilized. Many people passed us, who greeted us kindly with the Arabic word for "welcome," which sometimes broke from their lips with an energy that startled me; but the good impression made by this civility was counteracted by the manner in which they behaved to their women. It is women who carry the burdens, when there is no donkey to carry them; and it is a frequent sight in Syria to see a lazy Arab travelling along on a donkey, with two or three women trotting on foot beside him.

Our journey brought us to the top of an eminence, on the slope of which, eastward of where we stood, the town of Ramleh lay before us, the centre of a vast circle of huge old olive-trees, amidst which grew fields of luxuriant barley. A little without the terrace, in the midst of a quadrangle of ruined walls, arches, and vaults, two hundred feet square, stands a lofty tower of white marble with Saracenic arches. We entered the enclosure at its principal gate; a row of massive piers and vaults, partly entire and in part fallen, stood on each side of a spacious court, covered with fresh herbage. The ground beneath was hollow with pits, the vaults of which, in places, had fallen in. We descended by one of these openings, and found ourselves in a sort of crypt, spacious, and with lofty pillars supporting pointed arches. The sides of this subterraneous apartment are lined with a smooth stucco, and I have no doubt that it was once a reservoir into which the winter rains were gathered. There were two of them, one on the south and another on the north side of the quadrangle.

A man with a sabre by his side was sitting in the shade of the wall, as we entered the court, engaged in the usual oriental manner of passing time, that is to say, smoking a long pipe. He rose and followed us when we went into the vaults below; and when we came out, he kept near us: he was probably the keeper of the place. We ascended to the top of the tower by its narrow staircase; we heard his steps behind us, and while we looked at the glorious view from the summit, he seated himself near us and smoked his pipe tranquilly till we were ready to go down again. The atmosphere was beautifully transparent; the sea was in sight to the west; the mighty range of rocks which forms the greater part of the territory of Judea, bounded the view on the east; between these was the plain of Sharon—green and fresh, but no longer famed for its roses; still nearer lay the town of Ramleh, with its multitude of little domes forming the house-tops, and just under our feet was an Arab cemetery, crowded with tombs of a rude masonry, plastered over with mortar and whitewashed.

Our dragoman, in the mean time, had proceeded with the camels and the baggage to the Latin convent in Ramleh, which, on descending from the tower, we had some difficulty in finding. We wandered about in the outer streets of the town looking for it, until our appearance began to attract some attention. The boys shouted after us, and two of our party, lingering behind the others, were complimented with a volley of small stones, for which, however, the young rogues were rebuked by an elderly Arab. At length, we discovered our camels in a little enclosure, hedged with the prickly pear. Close at hand was the convent, to which we were admitted, and in which we found our rooms already assigned us. "I hope you like them," said the Superior, a Spaniard of prepossessing physiognomy and agreeable, courteous manners—"I hope you like them; they are the best we have."

In fact we had no reason to be dissatisfied; the day had been hot, and the coolness of our chambers on the ground-floor, vaulted with masonry, was very agreeable. Our cook had his convenient kitchen near us, with a small dining-room next it, and our attendants were provided with a spacious dormitory. The Franciscan convent at Ramleh, like most of the Latin convents in the castle, had but few inmates—there was but one friar besides the Superior, a Spaniard also, and with them was associated an Arab lay-brother, who had lived with them so long that he spoke Spanish fluently. The convent is a spacious building, erected round three or four different courts, all of them clean and silent. They told me that the convent was poor, which I thought not unlikely. While the bell was ringing for vespers, I happened to be in the main court, and looking round the corner, saw the gentlemanly Superior pulling the rope with great activity.

Our chambers swarmed with mosquitoes, bred in the numerous cisterns of the convent, containing rain-water, some of which were yet full to the brim, and open to the air. We had not been an hour in our beds before we wished ourselves again in our tents.

LETTER XIV.

Journey to Jerusalem continued.—We take our leave of the Arabs and their camels.—Journey on horseback.—Queer bridles and saddles.— A janizary of the American Vice-Consul at Jerusalem.—His long staff.—Entrance upon the hill-country.—A lunch under evergreen oaks.—Steep ascent by a bridle-path.—Sure-footed horses.—Soil full of loose stones.—Its fertility.—First sight of the Holy City.—The Jaffa gate of the city.—People promenading in the country.—Bearded priests.—Hotel kept by a Maltese.—Visit to the Church of the Holy Sepulchre.

JERUSALEM, PALESTINE, February 22d, 1853.

IN the morning when we left our rooms, we found the Arab camel-drivers preparing to return with their animals to their little town on the desert. Their journey ended here, and for each camel which they had led in their caravan from Cairo to Ramleh, the compensation to the drivers was about four dollars, to say nothing of a flogging or two thrown in, to sweeten the bargain, by our free-handed dragoman. We had been so long together in the solitude through which our journey lay, that we had conceived a sort of friendship for these people. We had found them respectful, laborious, and always ready with their services; and we now took leave of Mohammed and Mohammed Ali and Achmed, and the two others whose names I forget, with something like regret. The poor fellows seemed half-sorry to part with us, and Mohammed, the oldest and most responsible man among them, kissed the hands that were offered him to shake.

Meantime, a gigantic Syrian had brought to the convent-gate a troop of fifteen horses and mules, with which to perform the journey from Ramleh to Jerusalem. The horses were equipped with patched bridles, compounded of leather, worsted, ribbon, and rope, ragged saddles, and stirrups of various patterns, but principally of the Turkish, with a broad plate for the foot to rest upon. A janizary of the American Vice-Consul at Jerusalem, on his way home from Jaffa, had heard that there was a party of American travellers at the convent, and had come to offer us his company and protection during the rest of our journey. He wore a sabre, with a pair of pistols clumsily stuck in his sash, after the fashion of the country, and carried in his hand a long staff with a large silver head, the symbol of his office. We put into the hand of the Arab lay-brother, who spoke Spanish, the expected gratuity, and mounting our horses, proceeded through the streets of the town. Before us rode the janizary, resting his long staff on his Turkish stirrup, and occasionally wielding it to poke the people aside when they obstructed the way.

Crossing a rich plain, we entered upon a hilly country with frequent villages on the heights, and finally followed a road into a deep ravine, running far up into the mountain-country of Judea. At its bottom was a narrow bridle-path, choked with loose stones, and its steep sides were tufted with evergreen shrubs; on the right hand were olive-trees planted on terraces among the rocks, and on the left were flocks of goats, under the care of keepers, browsing among the cliffs. We made our mid-day halt at a spot where the ravine, widening, left a little valley, and a clump of evergreen oaks made a pleasant shade. Close at hand were the ruins of an old building—our dragoman called it a mosque, but I had little doubt it was once a khan, and that the spacious subterranean chambers, which were the only remarkable part of its remains, had once been reservoirs of rain-water.

Out of this ravine, after following it for a great distance, we climbed into an extensive plantation of olive-trees, by a path among the rocks, so steep, slippery, and obstructed with blocks of stone, that the attempt to travel it on horseback seemed to me scarcely less than an act of madness. I soon, however, perceived that there was no cause of fear. The horses of this country, though not otherwise a fine race, are wonderfully sure-footed, and pick their way in safety up and down precipices over which one of our own would infallibly break his neck.

We had a tedious journey up and down the bare hills, and across the stony valleys. The soil of Judea is everywhere full of loose stones, yet it seemed to me, from such examination as I was able to give, that the rocks of the country in disintegrating, resolve themselves into a rich mould, which, as soon as it is touched with moisture, starts into fertility. The barrenness that prevails is owing to the want of water; wherever that flows, the herbage is luxuriant, rich grasses spring up, and abundant harvests are reared.

At length, after crossing a bleak table-land, where the soil seemed to have been washed away by rains from the spaces between projecting rocks, we came in sight of the walls, the towers, and the domes of the Holy City. The ancient metropolis of Palestine, the once imperial Salem, had not lost all its majesty, but still sat like a queen in her place among the mountains of Judea. To the north stretched a broad grove of olive-trees, and under the western wall the green vale of Hinnom wound, deepening as it extended to the south, till it turned eastward to join the deeper glen of the Kedron; and eastward of the city were the steeps of Mount Olivet. I will not attempt the description of a place described so often, nor dwell upon the reflections which arose in my mind at the first sight of that spot from which the light of that religion now professed by all the civilized world, dawned upon mankind, and to which the hearts of millions in every zone of the globe yet turn with a certain reverence.

We approached the city by the road leading to the Yafa Gate, which at that hour—it was now nearly five o'clock—was pouring out its men and women to enjoy the last rays of a most pleasant sunshine. Among those who were walking into the country were small parties of young men in the academical garb of the Colleges, Armenian and Greek priests in their flowing black robes, and Latin priests in their brown gowns. I thought I had never seen so fine an assortment of beards of different tinges of color, as those which hung from those reverend chins. We entered the gates without being asked for our passports, and winding through narrow, dirty streets, and vaulted passages under houses which were built directly over the ways, we stopped at the door of the Melita Hotel, close to the Church of the Holy Sepulchre, kept by Antonio Zanieni, one of that race which is found everywhere dispersed through the East—the Maltese. We were shown into clean, comfortable rooms, after taking possession of which, we went to the church, where Greek mass was performing and the devout of the Greek communion were pressing to the place of the sepulchre, kneeling before it, and kissing the sacred stone in which it is enclosed. That evening, as the day was closing with great splendor of light and color, we heard the muezzin, from a minaret rising close to the church, shouting and quavering his proclamation of the hour of prayer, with extraordinary energy, as if he protested against the Jewish and Christian unbelief surrounding him on every side. Jeru·

salem is the resort of enthusiasts of every creed, and clime;—Jews, who are here to lament the destruction of their temple and wait for the coming of the Messiah; pilgrims and devotees of the Greek Church, the Latin and the Armenian, and religious adventurers from America, of the Protestant faith, who have crossed the Atlantic to assist in preparing for the return of the Jews.

Since we have been here we have visited most of the places within and without Jerusalem, associated by history or tradition with important events. We have just now returned from an excursion to the valley of Jordan and the Dead Sea, the narrative of which I thought to have given you. This letter, however, is already so long, that I have relinquished the design of writing out, at present, my notes of that journey. I have executed my principal purpose, which was to give an account of our passage through the desert and the southern part of Syria to Jerusalem.

LETTER XV.

The Lazaretto at Smyrna.—Beautiful harbor.—Fleet of American ships of war in the Levant.—Behavior of the Arabs to the Frank.—Relaxation of bigotry.—Mohammedan prejudices.—No Christian converts from Moslems.—Power of the foreign consuls.—Extravagant prerogatives of the American consuls.—Hasty appointments to consulships.—American missionaries at Beyroot.—Dr. Eli Smith.—Mr. Calhoun.—A Druse Emir.—Dr. De Forrest.—A girls' school.—Demand for educated wives.

SMYRNA, ASIA MINOR, March 29th, 1853.

THIS letter is written from the lazaretto of Smyrna, the great commercial city of the Turkish empire, seated on the borders of one of the finest harbors in the Levant. Before the long, yellow building in which I have my chamber, spreads a broad sheet of transparent water, remote from the agitations of the Mediterranean, and apparently surrounded by land like a lake. It is sheltered and overlooked in part by lofty mountains, with masses of forest on their sides, and summits of bare rock, and in part by green hills, up one of which the city has been climbing, of late years, from the low plain on the southern shore. Here whole navies might ride in safety, and never feel the storms that vex the open sea.

It is sometimes asked by Americans, why it is

that our squadron in the Mediterranean never makes its appearance in the waters of this excellent harbor. The design of maintaining vessels of war in this quarter of the world is, of course, to inspire respect, by creating an impression of our power to assert our rights against encroachment. A whole fleet of frigates anchored at Port Mahon or at Spezzia, would not have this effect in a much greater degree than if they were stationed at Brooklyn or Norfolk. Nobody makes a voyage to Port Mahon to admire the strength of our men-of-war, their capacity for speed, the excellence of their discipline, or the terrible beauty and perfection of their arrangements for dealing death upon our enemies. At Naples they are already so familiar a sight that their appearance does nothing to strengthen the impression already made. Our naval officers, at these places, interchange civilities with the people of the country, give balls on board their vessels, which are the admiration of the ladies, and do their best to make their time pass agreeably. But if the Navy Department would give a little attention to this matter, they might be employed to somewhat better purpose.

In a conversation on this subject, which I had with the American consul at Beyroot, he said, " In the event of any controversy arising between me and the Pasha here, it would be far more easily settled if there were an American vessel of war in the harbor." These words fully express the true use of the American squadron in the Mediterranean. The authorities of a barbarous country and an arbitrary government naturally pay as little attention to the rights of foreigners as to the rights of their own subjects, unless they find themselves forced to do otherwise. Let a nation bring the evidence of its strength and greatness to their doors, and their sense of justice is surprisingly quickened. A few years since, the English poured a storm of rockets and bombs upon Acre—Akka, as they now generally call it—and battered the fortifications and the town to fragments. Since that time the slightest complaint of the representatives of the English government has received immediate attention.

There is not a port of any consequence in the Levant which the American squadron ought not to visit in its turn. Here, at the principal centre of Turkish commerce, it might find a shelter in the most inclement season, and at Beyroot, the great port of Syria, with which our commercial relations are acquiring more and more importance, though the north winds in winter sometimes render the anchorage insecure, they would find the water as calm as a lake from the first of April to the first of November. The Turks will never be convinced of our power to exact satisfaction for injuries by what they read, for they never read; they must be convinced by what they see; and it is the proper business of our navy to instruct them on this point. The sight of our superb vessels, riding in their pride and strength upon the Turkish waters, would make the matter clear to their minds.

When our present consul first arrived at Beyroot, the Pasha was disposed to treat him as he treated the consuls of the minor powers, that of Tuscany, for example: he neglected to return his official call, a point of etiquette the strict observance of which is reserved for powers of the first and second rank. Our consul was not of a temper to submit to this, and wrote to the Pasha that if his call was not returned without delay, he should report the matter to the government of the Sultan at Constantinople. This had its due effect,—the call was returned. A short time afterward, the English consul at Beyroot gave an official dinner, at which the Pasha and the consuls of the foreign governments were guests, and at which the American consul was placed next to himself. A new light seemed to break on the Pasha's mind, and he afterward treated our consul with great consideration. But it is not fitting that the respect with which our country is regarded, should be left to depend on circumstances like these.

In the behavior of the people of this country toward the Franks, a great change has taken place within a few years. The ancient bigotry of the Moslems is fast relaxing. Not only do the Turks get drunk like Christians, of which I was sorry to see some examples on board the Austrian steamer that brought me hither from Beyroot, but they submit to contact with the Christians, and do not think themselves, as once they did, contaminated by it; and they suffer our presence in their most holy places. We had on board of our steamer a distinguished officer of the Turkish empire, Mohammed Pasha, the military governor of Damascus, a seraskier. There are but five seraskiers in the empire, and the office is equivalent to that of marshal in France. He dined with us occasionally, and his son always.

In Cairo, you may enter any of their mosques with a janizary, when the faithful are not at their devotions; at Beyroot you may enter them, if you will only take off your shoes. At Damascus, the idea that a mosque is profaned by the entrance of a Christian is still entertained, but even there the old fanaticism is giving way. "Ibrahim Pasha did a great deal of good when he was master of this country," said an old Jew waiter at the Palmyra Hotel in Damascus. "Before he came, no Frank, no Christian, no Jew, could ride on horseback through the streets; the Moslems would have pulled him down, and perhaps torn him in pieces. He was obliged to dismount at the city gate, and lead his horse through the streets. Ibrahim Pasha decreed that men of all religions should have equal privileges in the community. After Ibrahim Pasha was driven out, the English used their influence to keep for the Franks and Christians the rights he had granted them, and we are allowed to ride on horseback still."

This thaw of prejudices so strong and so long cherished, this disregard of the precepts of the Koran, encouraged as it is in high places, is very likely to become far more general in the next generation than it now is. There are some who think they see in it a sign of the approaching day, when the followers of Mohammed will have become gradually weaned from their false revelation, and be prepared to embrace a purer religion. There are others who imagine that this day has been postponed by the interference of the English in the controversy between Ibrahim Pasha and the Sultan. I was, not long since, at the Latin Convent on Mount Carmel, the procurator of which, Father Charles, an intelligent and agreeable man, is well known to travellers in Syria. "It was a great mistake of the English government," said he, " that it took the part of the Sultan against Ibrahim Pasha. The English fear that Russia may obtain possession of Constantinople. It was, without doubt, the ultimate design of Ibrahim, to seize upon the seat of the Turkish empire, and if it had once fallen into the hands of so able a prince, would have given England the barrier against the further advances of Russia, which she so much desires. But beyond all this, it was the policy of Ibrahim Pasha, as it was that of Mohammed Ali, his father, to break down the religious prejudices of the Mohammedans, to put all religions on a footing of perfect equality, to adopt European institutions, and to cause the Franks to be treated with courtesy and deference wherever they went. In this way, the gates of the East would have been opened to civilization and Christianity."

Meantime, I would not have you suppose that the old Mussulman hatred of the Franks, though so much diminished, is extinct. A sense of decency, or the fear of the bastinado, often restrains its expression in grown persons—for the foreign consuls, when an insult is offered to an individual of their nation, have the means of subjecting the offender to exemplary punishment—but it breaks out in the behavior of children, who feel no such restraints. I cannot say that I observed anything of this in Egypt, but it was apparent enough the moment we entered Syria.

As we passed through Khan Yoonas, the frontier town—a train of eight persons in the Frank costume, on camels—we were saluted by the boys and young girls from the open doors, the windows, and the house-tops, with shouts and gestures of derision. At Ramleh, a village one day's journey from Jerusalem, as our party were walking through the streets, two of them, lingering behind the rest, were followed by boys who threw stones at them, until they were stopped by an Arab coming out of his house, accosting them in an angry manner, and apparently commanding them to desist. I was one day walking near the Mohammedan cemetery, just without the walls of Jerusalem. It was Thursday, the day before the Mohammedan Sabbath; the women were praying at the graves of their friends. Two children—beautiful creatures they were—a boy and girl, with brilliant eyes, and gayly dressed, came forward from one of the graves, where two women were sitting, and sang, with great glee and spirit, a song current in the country, composed in ridicule of the Franks. At the entrance of the town of Nablous, in Samaria, where the women and children were assembled in hundreds, in their holiday dresses, in a beautiful olive-grove, the little stones thrown by juvenile hands rattled about us like hail, and we were pursued for a quarter of a mile by a chorus of shouts and songs, till we were fairly within the city gates. There are Protestant missionaries from America at Smyrna, at Beyroot, at Damascus, and other places, but they depend very much on the American consuls for protection. "We could not remain in Damascus," said one of them to me, " we could scarcely maintain ourselves here for a day, but for the support which is given to our rights by the vice-consul."

It is remarkable, as it is a proof of the almost ineradicable nature of Mohammedan prejudices against the Christians, in Syria, that the missionaries never attempt to make proselytes from among the professors of Islamism; they only seek to persuade to their faith those that belong to the Greek Church, or those who acknowledge the supremacy of the Pope. It is well understood that if a Mohammedan were to abjure his creed, and embrace Christianity, his life would be forfeited. "If the criminal tribunals did not meddle in the matter," said our vice-consul at

Damascus, " the people would, and we should have a tumult at once. There was, not long since, in this city, a Mohammedan who professed to believe the doctrines of Christianity, and who went to India, promising the missionaries to make a public profession of his faith in that country, but I know not whether he did so." The missionaries, it seems, do not insist upon the Moslems becoming candidates for the crown of martyrdom.

The foreign consuls in the Turkish empire have great power, under the laws of the country, and great weight with the government of the Sultan. If a Pasha or Governor of a province misbehaves himself, and gives them just cause of complaint, an application from them addressed to the Sultan is sure to procure his removal. "I can commit any man to prison, within the district for which I am consul," said our consul at Beyroot to me, " for any cause whatever; and it is only after he has been a prisoner for three days, that the Pasha has a right to send to me inquiring the reason of his detention."

But this is not all. A law passed by the Congress of the United States, in August, 1848, makes the American consuls appointed for the Turkish empire judges in all causes of a criminal nature, in which a citizen of the United States is the accused party. I pray you to look at the statute, and see if it is not an extraordinary one. The consul is both the judge and the jury, and from his sentence there is no appeal. The usages of the Turkish empire, and, if I am not mistaken, a special treaty with the Porte, sanction the exercise of this power on the part of the consul. Mr. Offley is the American consul at the port of Smyrna. He may not only throw me and the American friends who are with me, and the two Smyrniotes who came on with us from Cairo, and are now in this lazaretto, into prison and keep us there for three days, on no accusation at all, but he may hang all the Americans of our party to-morrow morning, without allowing us a moment's delay, or any opportunity of procuring the revision of a hasty or capricious sentence. If you should find the law to be as I have stated, I hope you will inquire whether it ought not to be immediately amended.

Powers like those which I have mentioned, ought not to be intrusted to any but the most able and upright men. An American consul in a port of the Turkish empire is the sultan of all the American citizens who are within his district; he holds their lives and liberties in his hands. As much caution ought to be used in selecting competent persons for the post, as for that of the most important judicial office—the highest conscientiousness and the soundest judgment are not qualities too exalted for it. Yet it is sometimes strangely misbestowed.

Not long since, a Prussian subject, who was obliged to leave Constantinople for some misbehavior, and who could not return to it in a private capacity, went to the United States, and after an interview with Mr. Webster, obtained from Mr. Fillmore the appointment of American consul at the port of Constantinople. He arrived at Syra, in Greece, with the commission in his pocket, and was waiting for an American vessel of war to convey him to his place of destination, where he expected to make a sort of triumphal entry, when Mr. Marsh, our minister at Constantinople, hearing of his appointment, wrote instantly to Mr. Fillmore, assuring him of the man's utter unworthiness, and advising that his commission should be immediately revoked. This was done, and the Prussian received notice of his dismissal as soon as it could be forwarded to him. I do not give you his name, because I am not quite sure that I remember it, and being in the lazaretto, have no means of informing myself by inquiry, but you may perhaps find it in the list of recent appointments; at all events you shall have it in my next, after I am let out of this prison. The case ought to be put on record as a warning against hasty appointments to office. I can hardly suppose that the office was bestowed, in this case, with any distinct recollection of its powers and responsibilities.

I have spoken of the American missionaries at Beyroot. They are learned and laborious men. One of them, Dr. Eli Smith, distinguished as an orientalist, is preparing, with the help of a well-educated native, a new Arabic translation of the Scriptures from the original languages, the one now used being from the Vulgate. Mr. Calhoun has a school for young men, at Abeih, on the western declivity of Lebanon, in which a regular course of four years' instruction is given, ending with some of the higher branches of mathematics and chemistry. All the pupils learn English, and some of them Greek. They are twenty-two in number, and one of them is a Druse Emir. Dr. Deforest has at Beyroot a girls' school of sixteen pupils, in which he is assisted by Mrs. Deforest. I was present at a part of the annual examination of this school. The girls acquitted themselves well in English composition—and the specimens of their drawing exhibited, did them great credit. They are clever geographers, I hear. They are from families of different denominations of Christians, and their parents, brothers, and sisters were present, their faces shining with the delight they felt at seeing their little friends becoming such accomplished scholars. The girls were neatly dressed; a spencer, or bodice, of printed calico, a skirt of the same material, but of lighter color, and a tarboosh or red cap, with a blue tassel, round the lower part of which was wound a gay-colored handkerchief, were the principal articles of their costume. They had mostly a healthy look, fine large black eyes, and large full lips. Some of them had a decidedly Jewish cast of countenance, though there were no Jewesses among them.

Both these schools are successful, and on them depend, I should suppose, the only hopes of the mission in Syria. The school for girls is so much in favor, that more persons apply for admission than can be received. As soon as the education of one of these girls is completed, her hand is immediately sought in marriage by some wealthy suitor. An impulse has been given to female education which is likely to spread over the whole country, and as mothers have, far more than fathers, the forming of the minds and dispositions of their children, may entirely change the character of the population, almost before the world is aware of the means by which the change is effected. The demand for female education has induced the Sisters of Charity, a Catholic order, to found a rival school, which I hear is largely attended.

LETTER XVI.

Constantinople.—Foreign relations of Turkey.—Arrival of Lord Stratford.—Feebleness of the Turkish government.—Corruption and public plunder.—Banditti at Smyrna.—Their robberies.—Their cruelties.—The Chiefs of the Banditti.—A Druse robber caught and caged.—The Druse population.—The Sultan.—His palace.—His Pashas.—Turkey held together by pressure without.

CONSTANTINOPLE, April 11th, 1853.

THE echoes of the Bosphorus and the Golden Horn—and they are very fine echoes—were awakened on the morning after my arrival at Constantinople, by a salute fired in honor of the arrival of Lord Stratford, the British Ambassador. It was quite time for him to be at his post, for the Russian government seemed on the point of bringing over the Sultan to its projects. What they were, I have learned from good authority, but perhaps before this letter reaches your hands you may have the information from some other quarter. Meantime, I give it to you, as nearly as I can, in the words in which I received it.

"The Russian government has pretended to interest itself very much in the dispute between the Greek and the Latin Church respecting the possession of the Holy Sepulchre and other sanctuaries in Palestine. It has also professed a strong desire to be recognized by the Sultan as a kind of protector of the Greek Christians within his dominions. These, however, were the public pretexts of a deeper design. Russia was in reality laboring to engage the Turkish government in a triple alliance, offensive and defensive, in favor of the principle of absolutism, with Austria for the third power. By means of this, it was hoped to mould the policy of the Porte to a perfect conformity with that of Russia, and to make it in effect a Russian province. You know that Turkey has been a place of refuge to the liberals of Europe from the persecution of the absolute governments; you know, too, that in Turkey perfect freedom of opinion concerning questions of European politics is allowed. This was to be so no longer, if the scheme of Russia could be carried into effect.

"The Sultan was not much inclined to the proposed alliance; the Grand Vizier was decidedly against it; but the Minister of Foreign Affairs, who had resided in western Europe, was as strongly in its favor. Pressed by his minister on one side, and the Russian embassy on the other, to make common cause with the two great absolute powers of Europe against the enemies of monarchy in its purity, there was danger that the Sultan would give way.

"Since the arrival of Lord Stratford, affairs wear a new face. The project of a triple alliance is now given up, and the negotiations on the part of Russia have fallen back upon minor questions. In resisting this project, the French government has been quite as decided and active as that of Great Britain, inasmuch as France has, or imagines she has, the same interest in preventing Russia from aggrandizing herself in the East."

In this account of the matter we have an explanation of the ordering of the French fleet to the waters of Turkey, the haste with which the British government despatched Lord Stratford to Constantinople, and the reported sailing—I do not yet know whether the report be true, but suppose it must be—of the British squadron at Malta for the Levant. The history of the affair illustrates in a remarkable manner both the weakness of the Turkish empire and the skill of

Russian diplomacy. The foreign policy of the Porte does not depend upon its own views or inclinations, but on the accidental influence which any of the great powers of Europe obtain over it. The Russian negotiators are the ablest and wiliest of Europe. Now, when they are just on the point of becoming by superior dexterity winners in the Turkish question, England tosses a sword upon the chess-board, and breaks up the game.

The Turkish government is as feeble in its administration at home, as it is in its dealings with other powers—feeble to enforce its own authority, feeble to preserve order, feeble to execute any work of public importance.

"The people who surround the Pasha," said an American, long a resident at Constantinople, "are the most rapacious and shameless of plunderers. No project on which money is to be spent can be set on foot, which they will not contrive the means of making an occasion of unbounded pillage. Not long since a road was laid out from this city to Adrianople and a large sum of money was raised for the purpose, enough, as was estimated, to complete it. Ten miles of the road was made, and the money was gone. It was computed that if the rest of the road were to be constructed at the same rate, it would bring the empire to bankruptcy, and the project was accordingly abandoned. Every public work is as wastefully managed."

While at Smyrna, the other day, I heard many accounts of robberies committed by banditti who have their haunts in the neighboring mountains. The city is fairly invested by them; and no man whose life is worth the ransom of a thousand piastres, ventures to trust himself at any considerable distance from the city, or to inhabit any of the neighboring villages, except that of Boornabat, on the plain of Smyrna. Yet in these villages many merchants still possess country-houses and gardens, grateful and pleasant retreats, where they once lived with their families a part of the year, when the heat made Smyrna, a closely-built city with very narrow and very dirty streets and not a single open square or public promenade, disagreeable and unwholesome. At present, they never visit them. Smyrna is now a sort of prison watched by a guard of robbers. About two years ago they seized Mr. Van Lennep, a respectable merchant of Smyrna, who was walking out with two of his children. They demanded a hundred thousand piastres for his ransom; which was negotiated down to fifty thousand—about twenty thousand dollars—on the payment of which, he was allowed to return home. One of the most remarkable of their recent captures was that of a Frenchman, the proprietor of a silk factory, who a short time since was by some means decoyed to a village not far from the city, seized, and released on the payment of thirty thousand piasters—about twelve thousand dollars. "He deserved his fate," said a Smyrniote, who acted as our guide through the city. "He had seduced several young women employed in his factory, and the people of Smyrna all say that the robbers served him right."

A lady, a native of the East, who had lived many years in Smyrna, related to me an incident which shows how little regard this community of robbers have for human life. "A young man of Smyrna, a Christian, had fallen in love with a Turkish girl, and eloping with her, sought refuge with the banditti, among the mountains. They gave him shelter, and urged him to become one of them, but he declined, hoping yet to escape to Greece or some of its islands, where to have run away with a Moslem would not be punishable as a crime. One day the chief of the troop renewed his instances, which were again firmly rejected. The chief drew one of his pistols, aimed it at the young woman, shot her dead on the spot, and turning again to her lover, said to him, 'Now you are ours.' Since that time the young man has been a robber. He knew that if he returned to society, the blood of the Turkish girl would be required at his hands."

The present chief of the banditti is one who, amidst the atrocities he is committing, has shown himself capable of generous actions. On one occasion, hearing that a member of a family in which he had been a servant was in some pecuniary embarrassment, he made his appearance and offered him the means of extricating his affairs, which, however, were not accepted. He resolutely withheld his companions from committing any robbery or act of wrong on Franks or Christians. "The Turks," he said, "are our tyrants and oppressors, and in plundering the Turks we perform an act of justice; but let us spare the Christians, who have never done us harm."

Some time since this man was taken and carried to Constantinople, where he was long detained a prisoner. During his confinement, the troop broke through the rules he had laid down, and robbed Franks, Christians, and Turks indiscriminately. "He is now at large," said the person who gave me this account, "and I hear that in returning to his companions he manifested great indignation at their conduct during his absence."

I expressed my astonishment that the Turkish government, having had him once in their hands, should have allowed him to be again at liberty.

"He bribed high," was the reply; "that is the way we explain such things in this country."

When I was waiting at Beyroot, about four weeks since, for the Austrian steamer to bring me to Smyrna, I heard that a Druse chief, a prisoner of the government, had been exposed at the barracks, without the city, chained to a post, with his hands tied behind him. On inquiry, I learned it was a Mohammed Daoud, a noted robber, who, for some time past, with a band of followers, has infested the road over Mount Lebanon, between Beyroot and Damascus, and committed many robberies and murders. They relate of him, that a man having a wife whom he coveted, he entered his house by night, slew the husband, and carried off the woman to his retreat in the mountains.

Mohammed Daoud was one of the boldest villains of his class. He wrote to the Turkish authorities enumerating the robberies and assassinations of which he had been guilty, and added: " You do not know by whom these things were done. I am the man—Mohammed Daoud; they were done by my hand or by my order. Take me if you can." The government had made various attempts to seize his person, but without success, until at length a Druse family named Joubelat, possessing high rank and great influence among their people, engaged to apprehend him and deliver him up. They watched his movements, and finding him at a convent, entered the room where he was dining. He asked them if they came in peace, and being told that they did, allowed them to approach him, and found himself their prisoner. He now complains that he was taken by treachery. He is to be taken to Constantinople, and if he has the means of paying a heavy bribe, I shall not be surprised to hear that he, like the robber-chief from Smyrna, is again at liberty, hovering about the road from Beyroot to Damascus.

While I am speaking of the Druses, I will add a word concerning those who inhabit the country to the south of Damascus, and their quarrel with the Turkish government.

These people possess a region, the passes to which among the mountains are easily defended by a few men. It is the rule of the Turkish empire to allow none to become soldiers in its armies who are not Mussulmen. The Mohammedans are subject to a conscription; the Christians, instead of this, pay a tax. The Turkish government says to the Druses, "We consider you as Mohammedans, and require of you a certain number of soldiers proportioned to your population." The Druses of Lebanon and Anti-Lebanon submit to the demand, but the Druses to the south of Damascus say, "We will pay a tax, but we will give you no soldiers."

For the present—for this year at least—the

quarrel has been compromised. In February the Druses said to the Turkish government: " We want time to attend to our crops : receive the value of a thousand yoke of oxen, and withdraw your troops the present year." The government, thinking it better to take the tribute than to get neither tribute nor conscripts, agreed to the postponement of the quarrel, accepted the conditions, and recalled their troops. The dispute meantime stands good for another season; it will be duly renewed, and the roads in that quarter will again become unsafe. It is possible that if the controversy is ever settled the Druses will make their own terms.

Last Friday—three days since—I saw the man who is the nominal head of that ill-compacted and scarcely cohering empire, once held in rigorous obedience by fierce and mighty monarchs, whose names were the dread of Christendom. From a wooden palace immediately on the Bosphorus—a finer is building for him, of marble, and of florid Palladian architecture—he rode forth, on a handsome black horse, a pale, slender man, dressed in a blue frock and pantaloons, wearing the tarboosh or red cap, which here, with the

French, has taken the place both of the hat and the turban. Before him rode his Pashas, his high officers of state and war, the men who dispose of the money that comes into his treasury— stout men, for the most part, with tolerably florid complexions. They were dressed in the same garb with himself. The enormous turbans and barbaric robes which officers of this class wore twenty-five or thirty years ago, are now only to be found in the Museum of Ancient Costumes, established by this Sultan's father in the Atmeidan or Hippodrome. As Sultan Abdool Medjid rode leisurely along, women who were standing in groups beside the way reached forth petitions wrapped in green silk, which were taken by some person belonging to the Sultan's train, and handed to an officer on horseback, carrying a box, in which they were deposited. It is said that the Sultan is always careful to read them. He is represented as a man of mild, amiable disposition, who would be glad to govern his empire better than he does, if he only knew how, or if those who surround him would only let him.

The different parts of the Turkish empire are now held together by the pressure applied to them from without. There are many who think it better that this should be so, than that its different provinces should be distributed among the powers of Christendom. For the interests of religious liberty it is most certainly better. The Mussulman government interferes less with liberty of public worship than most of the governments of Christian empires. To what degree civil and political liberty may yet be developed from amidst the elements now in effervescence in the Turkish empire, I will not undertake to conjecture, but I would as soon take my chance of freedom in Turkey as in most of the countries east of the British Channel.

LETTER XVII.

Beautiful view from the hill of Bulgoulu, near Constantinople.—Athens.—Corfu.—Glorious view from the Goruno.—Noble remains of ancient architecture at Athens.—Modern Greeks.—Their schools.—Their readiness to learn.—Syra.—The American consul.—Evangelides.—Dr. Hill's school.—Young ladies reading Homer in the original.—Dr. Jonas King, the orientalist.—His controversy.—His courage.—Anecdote of the American flag.—General dissatisfaction with the Greek government.—Corruption of public men.

Austrian steamer Imperative, on the ADRIATIC, between CORFU and TRIESTE, April 26, 1853.

THOUGH my visit to Greece has been a short one, I ought not to pass through so interesting a country without giving you a few notes of what I have seen and heard.

Within a few days past I have seen three of the most beautiful views in the world, all of them of different character. Just before leaving Constantinople, I made, with my companions, an excursion up the Bosphorus, the shores of which were noisy with the beginning of the mackerel fishery—people dragging full nets to land, with eager shouts, and men, women, and children, from the interior, hastening to the shore that they might secure their share.

In returning we stopped at Scutari, took

horses and galloped to the hill of Bulgoulu. As we ascended, the prospect opened upon us with new beauty at every step, until at last we stood on the summit in the midst of a scene of inconceivable magnificence and splendor. All Constantinople was at our feet, with its domes and sky-piercing minarets, dark masses of cypress, bright green fields, and blooming gardens, its shining waters sprinkled with sails, the winding Bosphorus, the Golden Horn, and the Sea of Marmora and its lofty islands; to the eastward, a country of cultivated fields and villages, and scattered dwellings; and to the south, rising above ranges of distant mountains, the summits of the Asiatic Olympus, white with snow. It was a scene, half the effect of which was owing to the extraordinary brilliancy and variety of the coloring.

In a few days afterward I was at Athens. I could not but acknowledge the beauty of the scenery which surrounds the city, but I missed something at first, which seemed necessary to its proper effect. The country, as some traveller says, is of the color of withered herbage. The soil, which is far from fertile, is almost white, and everywhere shows itself through the meager vegetation. The more, however, I looked, the more I admired—so varied and so harmonious were the outlines of the surrounding mountains. "The beauty of the place grows upon you," said one who had long lived at Athens, and I felt the truth of the remark every time I went out. In the aspect of nature here, there is that grand and severe repose, which, whether observed in the works of art or those of nature, makes the deepest and most durable impression on the mind.

We left Athens, crossed the Isthmus of Corinth, and took a steamer for the island of Corfu, the ancient Corcyra, a fertile and beautiful spot, its valleys and declivities shaded with old olive-trees, and gay, at this season, with innumerable flowers. "You should see the view from Goruno," said an English gentleman whom we met at our hotel. "Stanfield, the landscape-painter, declared it was the finest he had ever seen in any part of the world." We drove to Goruno and saw what might almost deserve the praise he gave it. Here was every element of the picturesque, both in color and form—mountain peaks, precipices, transparent bays, woods, valleys of the deepest verdure, and pinnacles of rock rising near the shore from the pellucid blue of the sea.

The remains of ancient art, which are to be seen at Athens, have the character of the surrounding scenery—repose and harmony. Of all that antiquity has left us in the way of architecture, they are the only ones which fill and satisfy the mind. Here is nothing too large or too little, no subordination of the whole to the parts —all is noble, symmetrical, simple; there is not a grace that does not seem to arise naturally out of the general design. It is wonderful how time has spared them. They are mutilated, defaced, and in great part overthrown, yet the marble, in many places, is as white as when it was hewn from the quarries of the Pentelicum Mount, and the outlines as sharp and clear as when the chisel had just finished its task.

All this destruction is the work of man, and but for human wickedness and folly the temples of the Acropolis would now be in almost as perfect a state as when Paul, in passing by, beheld the altar erected to the Unknown God.

In looking at these remains, one can hardly help asking himself whether the Greeks of that early age, which produced works of art wearing such a stamp of calm greatness and employing such a fine harmony of the intellectual faculties, were not of a different character from the Greeks of the present day. The modern Greeks are not wanting in capacity; on the contrary, they are exceedingly clever and ingenious, but they are restless and mercurial beyond almost any other family of mankind.

The schools of Greece are now flourishing, and crowded with pupils, whose parents deny themselves the necessaries of life that their children may be educated. We shall see in the next generation what are the influences of a general diffusion of knowledge upon a national character so volatile.

On our voyage from Constantinople to Athens, the steamer stopped for some time in the port of Syra, where we began a quarantine of twenty-four hours. I wrote a note to the American consul, Mr. Evangelides, a Macedonian by birth, educated in America, who came alongside of our steamer, and with whom we had a most interesting conversation. "I am satisfied," said he, "with regard to Greece. Her people are making the greatest sacrifices to acquire knowledge, and when this is the case, I expect everything. You see our town: those houses on the conical hill are Syra proper, those which cover the shore at its base form another city called Hermopolis. The place was a little village in the time of the Greek revolution; it has now a population of twenty thousand. Of these, three thousand are pupils in the different schools. In my own school are thirty-one boarders, of whom seventeen pay for their board and instruction; the rest are poor boys. In twenty years it will be hardly possible to find a Greek who cannot read."

Syra, you know, is but a little island on the Greek coast, and the city which bears that name owes its prosperity to its schools, which make it a place of resort not only from Greece, but from all parts of Europe and Asia, where the Greek race is found.

While at Athens, we visited the school in Dr. Hill's house, of which his lady was the founder, and had the principal management. The number of pupils is about three hundred. We were conducted through the different rooms by a Greek lady, educated at the school, who spoke English with great neatness, as well as fluency, and with just enough of a foreign accent to remind us that it was not her native language. The first department, or infant school as it is called, contained, I should think, fifty or sixty children of remarkably intelligent physiognomy. "These little creatures," said the Greek lady, "sometimes neglect their work, but never their lessons." They were taught, as were all the other classes, by assistants, who, with one exception, were educated in the school. Another department was called the ragged school, in which were one hundred and thirty girls distributed in different rooms. They were all children of the very poorest class, who were here taught reading, writing, mental arithmetic, needlework, etc. They were all of Greek families, with the exception of three German children, whom I distinguished from the rest at a glance by their fair complexions and quiet physiognomies.

In another part of the school were the children of persons in better circumstances, who were taught grammar, geography, English, and Ancient Greek. They rose as we entered, and, led by their teacher, a young lady, a native of Greece, sang a little hymn in English. In a yet higher class of young ladies, numbering about twenty, the studies are advanced to drawing, algebra, and other higher branches of education, and the study of Ancient Greek is continued with more critical exactness. I was now in a country where the young ladies

—Read in Greek the wrath of Peleus' son,

pass their graver hours with Plato, and, for light reading, turn the pages of Xenophon. I was shown a set of Greek classics, belonging to a young lady who assisted as a teacher in the school.

At this school, which is doing a vast deal of good, and which is constantly pressed with applications for the admission of pupils which it is obliged to decline or postpone, I heard the same account of the eager thirst of the Greeks for knowledge. "Offer a Greek child," said Dr. Hill, " a toy or a book, and he invariably chooses the book. He prefers the book to anything else you could give him, sweetmeats or coins, no matter what the value of the coin you offer may be. The Greeks," continued Dr. Hill, "are susceptible, in a high degree, of the influence of example, and with a proper system of education I should hope everything from them. The danger is, however, that in unlearning their superstitions, as they are doing, they may lay aside with them all reverence for religion, and all the restraints which religion imposes. I fear that this is the case with those who are educated at the government schools, and that these have made the Greek character worse instead of better, so far as their influence extends."

Notwithstanding this severe judgment, I cannot think that those whose desire of knowledge makes them submit to privations and hardships in order to acquire it are in a very bad way. They acknowledge and act upon a higher motive than the gratification of their appetites. They are learners in the school of self-denial, which is the basis of all virtue, and the only school in which an elevated character is ever formed.

While at Athens, I was curious to inform myself of the controversy in which Dr. Jonas King, the learned orientalist, has been engaged. He is a schoolmaster to the Greeks in another way, and, I believe, with equal success. You know he resides at Athens in the quality of a missionary. He preaches in Greek to a congregation of about thirty persons. The Greek constitution secures liberty of worship and speech on religious subjects, to persons of "all known religions." The law at the same time directs that no person shall revile the religion of another, and provides certain penalties against those who transgress this rule. Dr. King, in the exercise of the liberty guaranteed by the constitution, freely discussed the question of the adoration of the Virgin. His views were controverted, and he supported them by a pamphlet expressing no opinion of his own, but giving extracts, in the original Greek, from the fathers of the Greek church—Chrysostom, Basil, and others—in which they spoke of the Virgin as not a proper object of adoration. From this moment the controversy became a persecution on the part of his adversaries. He was arraigned on a charge of reviling the Greek Church. He employed able counsel, who undertook his defence on the ground that he had reviled no man's religion, but had merely expressed his own opinion on a religious question, with that freedom which the constitution allows. He was taken to Syra, in order to be tried, but the popular fury against him had been inflamed to such a pitch that it was feared that if he were landed he might be torn in pieces, and he was accordingly brought back to Athens. A principal reason of the popular excitement was the excommunication which had been fulminated against him by the Greek priesthood, denouncing him as a godless blasphemer, with whom all the faithful were forbidden to hold any communication, or to have the most indifferent transaction in life.

At length he was tried at Athens by the Areopagus. He was zealously defended by his counsel, but the court declared him guilty of reviling the Greek Church, and sentenced him to imprisonment. He was put into a dungeon with common malefactors—a dungeon so crowded, filthy, and damp, that, if arrangements had not afterward been made, allowing him to pass the term of his confinement, which was a short one, in the house of his jailer, his friends believe that he could not have lived to the end of it. A sentence of banishment was also pronounced against him, to which he has paid no heed. "If they come to carry me out of the country," said he, "I shall not resist, but until that is done, I shall remain."

It was during these proceedings that one Sunday a large crowd of Greeks, led by a priest of their Church, assembled in his house and garden to hear one of his discourses. His subject was the duty of religious toleration. At the close the priest asked a question concerning some things advanced in the discussion, to which Dr. King gave a prudent answer. The priest then demanded an explanation of certain positions laid down in another discourse, which Dr. King declined giving at that time, observing that he would agree to appoint almost any other day for the discussion. The multitude immediately joined the priest in demanding that the discussion should go on at that moment, with such fury and noise that his friends thought his life in danger. It happened at the time that the American consul was absent from Athens, and the functions of the office were delegated to Dr. King. An

American flag, a day or two previous, had been received by Dr. King, from Washington. In the midst of the tumult, at the very moment when the multitude seemed ready to tear him in pieces, he bethought himself of the flag, and hastily unrolling it, let it stream from one of the windows. As soon as the mob saw it, their clamors were hushed, they began to disperse in the utmost haste, and in five minutes not one of them was left in the house or the garden.

At present the triumph seems to be on the side of Dr. King. The Greeks are in a fair way to learn from him the lesson of religious toleration. He is under an ecclesiastical curse, as nobody can even speak to him without incurring the censure of the Church; yet everybody now speaks to him: he is exiled for his religious opinions, yet he remains at Athens, and preaches every Sunday without any reserve in the expression of his religious views. He has behaved throughout the whole affair with the greatest intrepidity, and, if we may judge from appearances, has brought his adversaries at last to the conclusion that their best policy is to let him alone. I admire his courage, and rejoice in his success.

On the steamer which took me from Athens to Calamaki, I had a conversation with one of those who led the opposition to the Greek administration, while an opposition existed. He spoke without any reserve on the subject of Greek politics. "The sovereign," he said, "has no sympathy with the Greek nation—has no interest in its welfare; he is still a foreigner, and only thinks of his equipages and his amusements. While there was an opposition in the Greek parliament to the administration, the complaint was that it prevented the enactment of measures for the public welfare: the opposition exists no longer; and yet nothing is done. Greece should have a respectable navy; her natural situation, with so many islands, peninsulas, gulfs, and harbors, should make us a maritime nation; yet we have no navy. We have but one vessel; we send out our young men to obtain a naval education in England, and when they return we have no employment for them. The Greek race throughout Thessaly, Macedonia, and Epirus are eager to break the chains of the Ottoman government, and join themselves to us; if we had a navy to show the Greek flag in their harbors, they would make the attempt, and the Porte would be compelled to submit. Our laws are unfavorable to commerce, yet commerce flourishes without them—a sign of what our trade and our commercial navy would be, if the laws were friendly, or even just to them.

"You see," he continued, pointing to a portly, healthy-looking gentleman in black, "you see there the king's confessor. That man has more to do with public affairs than all the Greek people. It is he who makes up the cabinet and bestows offices. Pay your court to him, and you may have what place in the government you please. It is by the conferring of offices that the parliament is managed. As soon as an able man appears, he is bought over from the people by being made a minister, or appointed to some other responsible post, in which he must give up his independence of opinion. You know how public men are corrupted. In Greece we are all poor, and are therefore the more strongly tempted."

Such are some of the topics of Greek politics

in the mouths of the opposition. What may be said on the other side, I had no opportunity to inform myself. I find myself at the end of my sheet, and, as I have little more to say on the subject of this letter, I will close.

LETTER XVIII.

May at Rome.—Abundance of flowers.—Severity of the Roman government.—The people kept quiet by the military.—Improved appearance of Rome.—The city beautified.—Copies of old pictures.—American artists at Rome.—Sculptors.—Painters.—Gibson's Venus.—Colored statues.—Powers at Florence.—The monument of Titian at Venice.

ROME, May 17th, 1853.

THIS is the season when, in Italy, the earth pours forth flowers with the same profusion as she offers her fruits in September. The gardens are one blush of roses, and the stronger-growing kinds of the rose-tree, both white and red, hang themselves on the walls with a surprising luxuriance of growth and bloom. The forest-trees yet cast a thin shade, but in the meadows the grass stands as high as it does with us in the middle of June, and is intermingled with numberless flowering plants. I rode out the other day to the lake of Nemi; the woody banks on each side of the road from Albano were colored with flowers, the apple-trees beside the way along the heights which surround the lake, showed their flower-buds just swelling with the spring, but in the deep basin below they were already fully open, and the white images of the trees were reflected in the tranquil water.

I wish there were no novelties to be observed at Rome more unpleasant than these. Every morning, at an early hour, the people of the city are awakened by military music, and the tramp of bodies of soldiery is heard as they march through the street. You meet them defiling through the public ways at other hours of the day; you see them performing their manœuvres and exercises in the public gardens; you hear the drum as often as the sound of bells; soldiers are more numerous in public than even priests. Every pains seems to be taken to let the people know that they live under a military government, which can afford to dispense with their goodwill. There are some circumstances, however, which tend to show that the government rules in as much fear as it seeks to inspire. Not a single copy of a journal from France or England is delivered from the post-office, till it is carefully examined to see whether it contains any political intelligence which the government chooses to keep from the knowledge of its subjects, or any political reflections of a nature which it disapproves. If these are found in it, the journal is withheld. A German, employed for the purpose, reads the English journals, and whenever he reports in favor of suppressing them they are destroyed. If the people stand in awe of the government, it is evident that the government dreads the people. There is distrust on one side, and hatred on the other—a condition of things which may last for years, but which, through a little imprudence on the part of the government, or a sudden exasperation on the part of the people, may, at almost any time, be exchanged for a state of open and bloody revolt.

In the midst of the evils of this false system of political organization, there are some tokens of prosperity to be seen at Rome. I have no doubt that the population of the city has considerably increased within the last twenty years. The proof of this is to be found in the rise of rents, and the difficulty which now exists in finding commodious apartments. I am told that rents have nearly doubled, and that the spacious suites of rooms which a few years since stood vacant in the palaces and other large houses, have now their inmates. This is owing, no doubt, in part to the general growth of the population of Italy during the late long interval of rest from war, and in part to the new facilities for travelling, which bring many more strangers to Rome than formerly, as visitors or residents. The tide, also, which in the ecclesiastical world is setting back toward the usages and opinions of the middle ages, no doubt floats many hither, and adds something to this new growth of Rome. Those who foretold that the Eternal City, in the unhealthy air of her Campagna, would at no distant day become unpeopled, must be content to look to a very remote and indefinite futurity for the fulfilment of their prediction.

Meantime the city is somewhat beautified with almost every succeeding year. Statues and columns are erected; the old irregular pavement of the streets, trodden with so much pain by those who had corns on their feet, has been taken up, and its place supplied by a smoother one, composed of small rectangular blocks of stone, like those used in paving the streets of Paris; a noble causey, with parapets and a pavement of hewn stone, has been lately made over the low grounds just without the gate, as the new Appian way;

and the public garden on the Monte Pincio has been embellished with rows of busts, in marble, of the illustrious men of Italy, her sages, artists, and authors. Workmen are now occupied in the garden, forming its walks, and planting them with trees, among which I perceive the evergreen magnolia, the bayonet-leaved palmetto, the date-palm, and other trees of the palm kind, which do not find the climate here too rude for their growth.

There is an occupation at Rome which, if I may judge from what I have seen and learned since I came here, meets with a very liberal encouragement from strangers—I mean the copying of old pictures. A great part of this, performed by native artists who make it their profession, is the merest and easiest journey-work. An American, the other day, bought a whole gallery of these copies, so ill-executed, I was told, that scarce anybody here would have allowed them to remain in his sight. These people forget that a good copy of a great picture is no common thing, and that it requires in him who works it, most of the requisites of a great painter. It is frequently said that a good copy is better than a bad original, which is true enough; but it should be remembered that good originals are not so very much more rare than good copies.

You may, perhaps, like some notices of what the American artists are doing in Rome. Crawford is occupied with his equestrian statue of Washington, designed for the city of Richmond. Around the principal figure, which is not yet fully modelled, will be placed statues of the contemporary great men of Virginia. Two of these, the statues of Jefferson and Patrick Henry, are already modelled, and plaster casts of them have been obtained. They are of colossal size, and are designed with a manly vigor and disdain of minor graces which quite delights me. If the rest of the monument shall be conceived in the same spirit, it will greatly raise Crawford's reputation. He has a small work under the chisel, the Babes in the Wood, which I hear has been ordered by a gentleman of New York. The children are lying hand in hand, and the redbreast has just began his pious office of covering them with leaves. The subject seemed to me beautifully treated.

The other American sculptors at Rome—Mozier, Richard S. Greenough, Rogers, and Ives, are all zealously pursuing their art, and occupied with works which show that there is not one of them who is not likely to surpass what he has already done. Mozier has a statue of Silence, which does him much credit; it is a female figure, standing in an attitude of command, with a calm severity of aspect, the forefinger of the left hand pointing to the lips. Greenough is modelling the figure of a shepherd, attacked by an eagle, which promises well.

Page is here, analyzing the manner in which Titian produced his peculiar coloring, and reproducing some of his heads in excellent copies. But he has done what is better than this; he has painted a portrait of Charlotte Cushman, a fine, solid painting, richly colored, with which not only his friends, but everybody who sees it, is charmed. Terry, a universal favorite with his countrymen, is occupied with a picture of "Samuel and his Mother." G. C. Thompson, who arrived here not long since, is looking at the works of the great Italian painters, and now and then making a clever copy of a head or a single figure. Nichols has very successfully transferred the calm glow of Claude's landscapes into some fine copies which he is making. Wotherspoon is luxuriating on the sylvan beauties of Nemi. For my part, I can hardly understand what an American landscape-painter, after satisfying a natural curiosity to see the works of the great masters of his art, should do in Italy. He can study nature to quite as much advantage at home—a fresh and new nature, as beautiful as that of Italy, though with a somewhat different aspect of beauty.

I was the other day in the studio of Gibson, the English sculptor. He showed our party a work in basso-relievo, representing Phaeton attempting to guide the chariot of the sun. It equals in fire and spirit anything the imagination could conceive of such a subject. The horses, with distended nostrils, plunge madly forward through space, seeming as if they would leap out of their harness, and the young charioteer holds the reins with an aspect of uncertainty and alarm. In another part of Gibson's studio was placed a statue, on which he had been trying an experiment that had long occupied his thoughts. The ancients, you know, colored or painted their statues, and this is supposed to have been done by persons who made it their particular profession. Gibson has a statue of Venus, a very pleasing figure, the hair of which he has colored of a very light warm brown, binding it with a fillet of the most delicate blue, stained the eye with a dim azure, with a tint of a crimson vein or two at the corners, laid the faintest possible bloom on the cheeks, touched the lips slightly with scarlet, and suffused the skin, over the whole form, with a carnation just perceptible, through which the blue stains of the marble appear like wandering veins. The drapery of the figure is left in the original color of the marble, except the border, along which runs a double stripe of pale blue, with another of pale crimson next to the edge. The effect is agreeable far beyond what I should have expected. The marble is deprived of all its appearance of hardness, and the statue has the look of a human figure seen through a soft mist; the outlines seem to blend with the atmosphere.

On my way hither, stopping at Florence, I visited the studio of our countryman, Powers. He had several busts lately executed with his usual skill in giving the expression of character and life, and was then occupied with a figure intended as a representative of our new state, California. In her left hand she holds a divining-rod pointing downward to the mines in her soil, and in her right she conceals behind her back a scourge, intended as an emblem of the calamities which follow the eager search for gold. Powers at present models his figures in a peculiar manner. He builds them up with fragments of dry plaster, cemented by the same material in a liquid state. When any part of the figure requires to be made rounder or fuller, he lays on the plaster with a flexible gutta percha trowel; when it is to be reduced in size, he applies a kind of file or rasp, of which he is the inventor, which never becomes clogged, and is pierced with holes, through which the plaster shoots in a shower. In this manner he completes the model in a shorter time than it could be moulded in clay, and avoids the trouble of taking a cast.

While I am speaking of works of sculpture, let me mention the monument of Titian, at Venice, in the church of Santa Maria dei Frari, erected last year,—more than three hundred years after his death. It stands among the monuments of the statesmen and warriors, the admirals and doges of Venice, as lofty and as splendid as any of them, and in a taste less barbaric. Near the base sit two colossal figures—on the left a bald old man, with eyes closed, representing Time Past, holding a tablet, on which are inscribed the words of the Emperor Charles V., uttered in 1506, commanding that Titian be made a knight and count of the empire; on the right a man in the vigor of life, representing Time Present, with a tablet, on which is engraved the command of Ferdinand of Austria, in 1853, directing a monument to be erected to Titian's memory. Titian sits on the summit of the pedestal, unveiling with his right hand the statue of Isis, or Nature, and laying his left on a volume brought him by a winged youth,—intimating that he derives the inspiration of his aid from the two sources of nature and religion. On each side of him stand two allegorical figures, one of which, the Muse of Painting, looking forward with lifted eyes as if into the distant future, brings him the wreath of immortal fame. On the wall of the monument, and under the arch over the head of Titian, is beautifully sculptured, in basso-relievo his noblest work, the Assumption of the Virgin; and four other paintings of his are copied in the same manner, on a smaller scale, in different compartments. On the top of the arch, forty feet from the floor, stands the winged Lion of St. Mark, the emblem of that Venice for whose churches and halls his finest paintings were produced. This monument is the work of Luigi and Pietro Zandomeneghi, and strikes me as one of the finest things of its kind in Venice.

LETTER XIX.

Fresnel lights.—Their strength and brilliancy.—Improvement in their construction.—Tomb of Napoleon.—Its magnificence.—Imperfect civilization of mankind.—Exhibition of the works of living artists.—Naked Venuses.—Ugly head of Louis Napoleon.—Duveau.—Death of Agrippina.

PARIS, June 1st, 1853.

I HAVE just returned from a visit to one of the government offices, in which the Fresnel lights, designed for the light-houses on the French coast, are deposited. The invention of Fresnel is one of the most beautiful examples we have of that skill by which the apparently barren phenomena of science are forced into the service of man.

Light, you know, radiates in all directions. Place a lamp in a tower on a sea-coast, and part of its rays are wasted on the clouds above it, part on the earth below, and part stream to the right and left, where they are not wanted. By a most ingenious arrangement of prisms, Fresnel collected these useless rays and sent them forward in a horizontal direction, parallel with the surface of the ocean, where they must meet the eye of the mariner. An intense light, by this concentration of its beams, is obtained from a single lamp. I desired to see an example of the effect produced, and a lamp was placed within one of Fresnel's circles of prisms, while I stood at the distance of twenty feet or more. It blazed into my eyes like the rising sun, and I could not bear to look at it.

Lieutenant Bartlett, of the United States Navy, is now in Paris, superintending the purchase of two or three of these lights, for which appropriations have fortunately been obtained from Congress. One of them is shortly to be sent out to America, and will, it is expected, be exhibited for a time at the Crystal Palace. I hope it will be so placed that everybody may see it without cost; for I regard it as a matter of great importance that the perfect manner in which the invention fulfils its purpose should be generally known and acknowledged. The want of good lights on our coast is a scandal to our country. France, with a much smaller marine commerce than ours, has erected Fresnel lights at every part of her borders on the Atlantic and the Mediterranean where the seaman needs the least notice of danger.

These strong rays, piercing the fogs and storms, give the necessary warning in any state of the weather. England, with a commerce but little larger than our own, has also adopted the Fresnel lights. We, on the other hand, content ourselves with putting up a few lamps, which glimmer feebly when the air is clear, and are of no use in thick and foggy weather—that is to say, when their light is wanted. We might nearly as well let our light-houses fall to ruin, and imitate the example of Turkey, which leaves its whole coast in entire darkness.

One or two of the Fresnel lights have already been set up in America, but they are of the original early pattern—before Fresnel and his brother had perfected the invention. I saw one of these at the repository of which I am speaking, and the difference between it and those which are at present used in France, is very great. In that model, Fresnel employed only prisms with straight sides; he had no apparatus for making any other; they were put together in small pieces; the light was obstructed by the cement used to confine them in their places, and the stray beams of light which escaped through the space between the prisms, were caught upon mirrors and reflected in the desired direction. But in the new Fresnel lights, the mirrors are laid aside as no longer necessary; the prisms have taken a curved shape; they are larger and less numerous, and the sphere of glass which they form, enclosing the lamp, is of a far simpler and more solid construction, and a more perfect transparency.

I was taken afterward to the workshop where these prisms are made, and whence the western coast of Europe is supplied with the apparatus for its light-houses. Here large wheel-shaped masses of glass, fixed upon tables revolving horizontally, were ground with sand to the proper angle, and finally polished. In another part of the building artisans were at work, framing the turrets of metal and glass in which the apparatus of Fresnel is enclosed. These are roofed with copper, and the iron ribs in which the glass is set are covered on the outside with thin copper bars, so that no part of the iron is in danger of corrosion by being exposed to the external air.

The great advantage of Fresnel's apparatus

lies in the strength of the light which it throws in the direction where it is wanted, but it has two other important recommendations—its economy, and the ease with which it is kept in order. With a single lamp it does what in the old method required thirty, and it dispenses altogether with the clumsy contrivance of reflectors, which are constantly becoming tarnished and wearing out. The supply of oil which is needed is, of course, comparatively trifling. I hope, for my part, that no time will be lost in lighting the whole coast of the United States, through all its degrees of latitude, both on the Atlantic and the Pacific, with the apparatus of Fresnel. The outlay at first would be considerable, but it would be soon made up to the treasury in the diminished expense of maintaining the lights. A liberal appropriation for the purpose made at once, would be an act of the highest frugality for the public treasury, to say nothing of the lives it might preserve, and the cargoes it might save from wreck.

I have been told that Captain Forbes, of Boston, not long since took out with him to America two ship-lanterns constructed on Fresnel's plan.

They were found to answer their purpose admirably, as I hear, but the Yankees, with their usual dexterity in applying such resources as they have at hand, immediately hit upon a substitute for Fresnel's prisms of cut-glass, which is a great deal cheaper and succeeds almost equally well. They form the glass into prisms, with the necessary curve, by pressure, and in this way construct a lantern but very little inferior in the strength of its light to those made in the French way.

The other day I went to the church of the *Invalides*, to see the tomb of Napoleon, which has been several years erecting, at an immense cost, and is just completed. There is not on earth so magnificent a mausoleum as that which is destined for the remains of the former Emperor of France. On entering the church I found myself in the midst of a throng hastening in the same direction, and saw before me, at the opposite end of the building, a large altar, blazing with gold, under a gilded canopy, which rested on twisted pillars of black and white marble. In front of it, immediately under the windows of the dome, appeared a circular balustrade of white marble, around which the people were pressing. I joined them, and saw that it enclosed a broad, open space, sunk, perhaps, fifteen feet below the church. There, on a pedestal of blue granite, stood an enormous open sarcophagus of polished porphyry, the lid of which lay near it, on a machine, ready to be slid over it as soon as the ceremony of sepulture shall be performed. On the pavement below, around the pedestal, was a wreath of laurel leaves and berries, wrought of various-colored marbles—among which a vivid green marble, from the quarries of the United States, was conspicuous. Surrounding the sarcophagus, and standing against the pillars which support the floor, was a circle of colossal figures in marble, the meaning of which I did not attempt to study. One of them, a winged figure, with a trumpet by his side, was perhaps the angel of the resurrection, who is to summon the great warrior from his grave on the day of account, when he will be unpleasantly confronted by the multitudes who were slain in his wars. In the recesses behind these statues were sculptures in bas-relief, representing some of the most important events of Bonaparte's history.

In that sarcophagus is soon to be placed the handful of dust which is all that remains of one who, for a few years, was the terror of the world. In its material, its form, and its glittering polish, this massive receptacle reminded me of the huge chests of porphyry found in the newly-opened tomb of Apis, at Sakkara, enclosing the bones of the sacred ox of Egypt. It is thus that, in different ages of the world, the same posthumous honors are paid to a quadruped and a conqueror, by two nations, each claiming in its day the palm of civilization. The Egyptians were the nearer right of the two; they honored the representative of a most useful tribe of animals; the French pay their homage to one whose title to it is, that "with infinite manslaughter" he won an empire which he was not able to keep.

I regretted that I could not look at the sculptures in relief below, except at a distance: they will be accessible, it is said, as soon as the remains of Bonaparte are inurned. I inquired of a friend residing in Paris, when this would be done. "There is a controversy," he replied, "about this matter among the Bonapartists. One party insists that the heart of Napoleon shall be deposited by itself in the church of St. Denys, among the monuments of the former sovereigns of France; but Jerome swears that he will not allow his brother's body to be cut up in that manner. The ceremony of removing his remains to the sarcophagus has, therefore, been postponed for a year."

But we had not yet seen the whole of the monument. Passing beside the glittering altar, we descended a flight of steps to the level of the great Court of the *Invalides*. Here, immediately back of the altar, and under it, I saw the entrance to the tomb, a massive doorway, over which are engraved the words of Napoleon expressing his desire to be buried among the French people on the banks of the Seine. On each side of this passage to the sarcophagus stands a colossal figure, in bronze; one of them bearing, on a cushion, a globe and sceptre, the symbols of dominion, and the other a sword and gauntlet, emblematic of the violence by which that dominion was gained, and, for a brief space, upheld. As we were considering these figures, the voices of priests and a choir, chanting at the altar above, resounded up the lofty dome; it was a litany, nominally addressed to the God of Peace. I looked about me, and saw only the symbols of warlike glory, and encouragement to the pursuit of renown in arms. On the walls were the sumptuous monuments of men who had distinguished themselves as the instruments of warlike ambition and conquest—Vauban, Marshal Bertrand, and others. This church itself had been converted into the mausoleum of a conqueror; it was the shrine of Napoleon; this altar formed a part of his monument, and this hymn, whatever its words, was chanted in his honor. I had before me one of the forms in which the Power of Destruction is still worshipped. What a groundless fancy, to suppose that the adoration of a Great Spirit of Evil has become extinct with the race of ancient Persians, or exists only among a few savage tribes! I left the place with the throng, passing out to the street through the Hospital of the *Invalides*—for we were not permitted to retrace our steps to the principal entrance. I left it with a strong impression of the yet imperfect civilization of mankind.

An exhibition of the works of living artists is now open in this city. It contains more than twelve hundred paintings, three hundred and twenty works of sculpture, and two hundred and sixty engravings and architectural designs. These are not half the number of works offered by the artists; about twenty-five hundred were rejected by the committee employed to make the selection, and among these were some which at least deserved a place among the best which were accepted. There was no artist on the committee; those who were named as members declined to serve, and the politicians and public men who finally composed it were probably not the best judges in such matters.

I hope so at least, for the collection is far from being as good as I expected to find it, and I should be glad to believe that it would have been better if the task of selection had been intrusted to a better committee. In the department of sculpture, the want of a high standard of art is perhaps most observable. There are plenty of naked Venuses and nymphs, simpering, leering, and sprawling; and these are oddly enough contrasted with several figures of female saints, wearing an air of theatrical and resolute prudery. An Egyptian maiden stooping with a look of compassion and tenderness to take the infant Moses from his ark of rushes, is one of the few female statues not strictly ecclesiastical which is not vulgar. Of the busts there are some good ones, but many of them have a sort of smirk or an affected attitude. There are several attempts to make something of the head of Louis Napoleon in sculpture, but the subject seems an intractable one, and none of them are successful.

There are many historical pictures—some of them very large, and scarce any of the large ones tolerable. The largest is by Matout, representing Ambrose Paré applying, for the first time in the annals of surgery, the ligature to the arteries of a lamb, after an amputation—an immense failure. The subject is coldly and confusedly treated. The best of this class is the *Death of the Virgin*, by Lazerges, a subject which the painter has managed with dignity and feeling, though the dignity, I must say, rather predominates. The death-struggle is just past, the household stand in sorrow around the couch of the dead, whose countenance wears the tokens of a happy departure, and a little child is advancing, encouraged by its mother, to lay a handful of roses by the Virgin's calm cheek. You may judge of the strange sort of things to be seen in this gallery, by what I shall tell you of the *Death of Agrippina*, by Duveau. A large, elderly woman, of a livid complexion, is sitting up naked in her bed, and throwing her arms abroad in the air, facing three half-clad ruffians, with complexions of reddish brown, who rush at her with clubs and daggers, while a scowling maid-servant, behind her mistress, is huddling on her garments, which seem to refuse to cover her. I must not omit to mention a picture by Winterhalter, representing Florinda and her Maidens beginning to disrobe her for the bath, which is very beautiful. Of the landscapes, there are none very remarkable; the best are those which are apparently studied from nature; the larger and more elaborate ones seemed to be painted in forgetfulness of nature. There are portraits in the collection, good, bad, and indifferent; the indifferent forming the largest number.

After all, I am making a criticism which must be the universal one in regard to all miscellaneous collections of the kind. The greater number of the works produced by artists in all ages are unsuccessful, or but partially successful, endeavors after excellence. The works which survive to be the admiration of succeeding times are few in any single year, and in the most prolific years form an exception to the mass of works produced.

www.ingramcontent.com/pod-product-compliance
Lightning Source LLC
Chambersburg PA
CBHW032008230426
43672CB00010B/2285